Understanding Social Work

Other books by Neil Thompson

Practice Teaching in Social Work (with Osada, M. and Anderson, B.)
   (second edition)
Crisis Intervention Revisited
Existentialism and Social Work
*Anti-Discriminatory Practice** (third edition)
Dealing with Stress (with Murphy, M. and Stradling, S.)*
Age and Dignity: Working with Older People
Theory and Practice in Human Services (second edition)
*People Skills** (second edition)
Meeting the Stress Challenge (with Murphy, M. and Stradling, S.)
Child Protection: Challenge and Change (co-editor)
*Promoting Equality** (second edition)
Stress Matters
Tackling Bullying and Harassment in the Workplace
Understanding Social Care (with S. Thompson)
Loss and Grief: A Guide for Human Services Practitioners (editor)*
Building the Future: Social Work with Children, Young People and
   Their Families
*Communication and Language: A Handbook of Theory and Practice**
Partnership Made Painless (with Harrison, R., Mann, G., Murphy, M.
   and Taylor, A.)
Group Care with Children and Young People (second edition)
Community Care (with S. Thompson)

* Also published by Palgrave Macmillan

Understanding Social Work

Preparing for practice

Second edition

NEIL THOMPSON

CONSULTANT EDITOR: JO CAMPLING

palgrave
macmillan

First published 2005 by
PALGRAVE MACMILLAN
Houndmills, Basingstoke, Hampshire RG21 6XS and
175 Fifth Avenue, New York, N.Y. 10010
Companies and representatives throughout the world

PALGRAVE MACMILLAN is the global academic imprint of the Palgrave
Macmillan division of St. Martin's Press LLC and of Palgrave Macmillan Ltd.
Macmillan® is a registered trademark in the United States, United Kingdom
and other countries. Palgrave is a registered trademark in the European
Union and other countries.

ISBN-13: 978 1–4039–4202–9 paperback
ISBN-10: 1–4039–4202–1 paperback

This book is printed on paper suitable for recycling and made from fully
managed and sustained forest sources.

A catalogue record for this book is available from the British Library.

10   9   8   7   6   5   4
14   13   12   11   10   09   08   07

Printed in China

For SSDB

Contents

The author

Neil Thompson has over twenty-seven years' experience in social work as a practitioner, manager, educator, author, editor and consultant. He has been Professor of Applied Social Studies at Staffordshire University and has also served as a Visiting Professor at the University of Liverpool and North East Wales Institute (University of Wales). He now works as an independent trainer and consultant with Avenue Consulting Ltd (www.avenueconsulting.co.uk), a company he established in 2000. He was also responsible for setting up the *humansolutions* self-help website (www.humansolutions.org.uk).

Neil has over 100 publications to his name, including best-selling books, papers in learned journals and training and open learning materials. He is the editor of the *British Journal of Occupational Learning* (www.traininginstitute.co.uk) and has been involved with a number of other journals. He is the series editor for the *Theory into Practice* series of books published by Russell House Publishing.

Neil has qualifications in social work; management; training and development; and mediation and alternative dispute resolution, as well as a first-class honours degree and a PhD.

Neil has been a speaker at conferences in the UK, Greece, Norway, the Netherlands, Canada, the United States and Australia. He is a Chartered Fellow of the Chartered Institute of Personnel and Development and a Fellow of the Institute of Training and Occupational Learning. In addition, he was elected as a Fellow of the Royal Society of Arts for his contribution to workplace learning.

His website address is: www.neilthompson.info

Preface to the first edition

This book represents an attempt to develop an overall picture of what social work is; how it is carried out; what its practitioners need in order to be effective; what is (and is not) good practice; and what obstacles stand in the way of good practice. It is, inevitably of course, a personal view, but one which is grounded in over two decades of experience in social work as a practitioner, manager, educator and consultant. It is not intended as a definitive statement on social work, but rather what I hope will serve as the basis for much discussion and debate about the important range of issues covered.

My current role involves me in teaching social work students as part of their professional training; running in-service training courses for experienced practitioners; serving as an external assessor for a number of social work courses; acting as a consultant to social work and related agencies; acting as an expert witness in legal proceedings (for example, where clients are suing a social work agency); and writing and editing a range of social work publications. This diverse career profile brings me into contact with a wide range of people in the social work world and enables me to have insights into many aspects of policy and practice. This means that I regularly come across examples of practice that range from good to excellent, and this is a heartwarming part of my work. However, it also sadly brings me into contact with more examples of bad practice than I would like to see, which is something that I find very disheartening. This book is therefore intended as a contribution to making sure that the good and excellent practices continue to flourish, while the bad practice becomes less common.

Social work is a challenging occupation. It is one that is subjected to much criticism and even vilification. None the less, there is still a significant 'army' of practitioners who continue to struggle on, committed to doing what they reasonably can to make a positive contribution to social welfare and social justice. Each year new groups of students begin their studies to work towards becoming qualified social workers, prepared to invest considerable time, effort and energy into learning and developing. They begin a major undertaking, but most are aware that they are entering a profession that offers considerable rewards and satisfactions as well as major challenges, demands and dilemmas.

This book does not offer any magic solutions to the problems faced in social work or any guarantees that the rewards will be forthcoming. More realistically, what it does offer is a picture of social work as an occupation which is difficult and demanding but none the less worthwhile, if not essential, as part of a society based on humanitarian values. I hope that this book will help to make the demands and challenges more bearable and the positive value and contribution of social work more apparent.

NEIL THOMPSON

Preface to the second edition

It has been very gratifying to see the first edition of this book establish itself very quickly as a popular and successful text. What has pleased me most about the very positive feedback I have received is that the book appears to have done what I wanted it to do – that is, to show social work as it really is: a professional undertaking which brings with it a mixture of difficult, demanding and frustrating situations and the satisfying rewards of making a positive contribution to tackling individual problems, needs and distress while also playing a part in the broader process of promoting social justice and humanitarian values. 'Nobody said it was going to be easy' is a refrain I find myself using a great deal in my conversations with social work staff and managers. Social work is certainly not easy, but that is what makes it challenging and thus potentially rewarding. I am delighted that the first edition seems to have succeeded in getting that message across.

In the five years since the first edition there have been a number of significant changes in social work education. The Diploma in Social Work, for so long the mainstay of social work education, is now being superseded by the degree in social work. This is a development I very much welcome. After twenty years in social work education, I am only too aware of the limitations of trying to fit everything needed for good practice into two years of study. The new degree not only gives greater scope for addressing the complexities of social work, it also gives a very clear message that social work is a professional activity – one that is worthy of a significant investment of time, effort and money, and one that requires a high level of professional knowledge and skill.

The intervening period between the two editions has also seen the introduction of National Occupational Standards and Codes of Practice, as well as the beginnings of the process of professional registration of social workers – all important steps in the process of affirming and consolidating social work's professional status.

However, despite these changes, the book's 'messages' remain the same, primarily the argument that: social work is difficult, but it is also very important and worthwhile. I hope that this new edition will continue to play a part in helping to clarify what social work is all about as a guide for those considering a career in social work and for those already 'in training' and as a 'refresher' and reaffirmation for those who have been involved in the profession for some time.

The new edition contains no major changes. Producing the revised text has involved incorporating the changes in social work education, updating the recommended reading sections, adding a few additional points at various places in the text and adding a guide to internet resources at the end. I hope you will find the book of value and that it will help you in deciding whether social work is for you and/or being clear about what is involved in good practice and why this is important.

NEIL THOMPSON

Acknowledgements

This book, in both its incarnations, represents in some ways a summary of my learning about social work over my career to date. This means that the number of people I am indebted to would form a much longer list than I can realistically present here. I must therefore confine myself to thanking in general the very many people over the years that I have learned so much from, and restrict the specific thanks to a much smaller range of people.

Colin Richardson, Fellow of Keele University, has been a significant influence on my development over the years, for which I am very grateful, and his influence continues to be felt here due to the helpful feedback he gave me on an earlier draft. Denise Bevan, of St Rocco's Hospice, is a friend and colleague whose support and friendship I value enormously. I am grateful to her for providing helpful comments on an earlier draft of this book and for her affirmation of its value. I am pleased to be able to say a big thank you to Judy Marshall for her excellent copy-editing work.

Jo Campling once again deserves thanks for her continued support, as do Catherine Gray, Beverley Tarquini and Sheree Keep at the publishers. And, finally, I must record my immense gratitude to Susan Thompson. As with my previous books, she has been a major source of support in so many ways. I owe her so much.

Introduction

Despite the very demanding nature of the job and the frequent media criticisms, the level of interest in social work as a career has remained relatively high over a long, long period of time. When student grants were replaced by loans, the level of applications for places on courses understandably fell, but has steadily built back up again. A recent recruitment drive, with its slogan of: 'Social Work. It's all about people. It's that simple and that complicated', has no doubt fuelled further interest in this fascinating and puzzling occupation. Clearly, it is a type of work that brings many rewards, but also brings with it many demands and challenges. This book has been written to provide a picture of what is involved in social work so that:

- people considering a career in social work can develop an understanding of what the social work role entails – the tasks, duties, pressures and pleasures;
- social work students seeking a professional qualification can use it as a guide and foundation for their studies;
- newly qualified workers can use it as a guide and resource to help them make the transition from social work student to qualified and established practitioner;
- practice teachers, training officers and tutors can use it as a resource in supporting students through their studies;
- experienced workers can use it as an opportunity to revisit their 'roots' as a source of affirmation; and
- people involved in the helping professions more broadly can develop a clearer understanding of what often appears to outsiders as the mysterious world of social work practice.

It is important to stress, right from the start, that a book such as this will inevitably reflect the author's own values, preferences and perspectives – my own conception of what social work is or should be. Clearly, others will have different perspectives and viewpoints, and will not necessarily share my views. However, I have tried to make my views and values explicit where possible so that what I have to say is not presented as a definitive statement that readers can take or leave. Rather, it is to be seen as a starting point for understanding, further study, debate and analysis. That is, my intention is to help facilitate understanding and appreciation of the complex nature of social work, rather than to provide ready-made answers. Indeed, a recurring theme of the book is that there can be no ready-made answers – social work is a process of 'tailoring' solutions to fit particular circumstances, rather than providing 'off the peg' responses.

The very nature of social work, and many of the concepts that underpin it, is *contested*. That is, there is no definitive consensus and many competing schools of thought. It therefore has to be recognized that this book should be seen as being more about opening a debate than closing one.

Chapter 1 begins by exploring 'differences and commonalities', and, in doing so, seeks to establish what is specific to social work and what it has in common with the other human services or 'helping professions'. This involves wading through some fairly complex issues, but we are none the less able to identify a number of clear pointers to help make sense of what social work is and how it relates to other occupations and disciplines.

Chapter 2 is concerned with the legal and policy context in which social work operates. Social workers do have a degree of autonomy, but what they can or cannot do – and what they *must* do in certain circumstances – depends to a large extent on a number of laws and the policies that relate to them. Our task, in Chapter 2, then, is to develop at least a basic understanding of how law and policy relate to social work practice, and just how significant they are.

A knowledge of law and policy is not the only knowledge base social workers need. Indeed, the knowledge needed is quite extensive, covering aspects of psychology, sociology, social policy and philosophy, as well as specific social work theories and methods. This knowledge base is the subject matter of Chapter 3, as we examine the building blocks of formal knowledge and theory on which professional practice is based. The main focus of the chapter is the identification of what knowledge is needed and why such knowledge is important, if not essential.

Of course, knowledge is not enough on its own – social workers also need a set of skills. The skills involved are many and varied, and so

Chapter 4 provides an overview of this skills base. It begins with a discussion of the competences identified by the former governing body for social work education, the Central Council for Education and Training in Social Work (CCETSW) and the key tasks identified in the recently published National Occupational Standards for Social Work. However, what will also be emphasized is that the skills involved in social work go far beyond these basic competences.

Chapter 5 is based on the argument that the contents of the previous chapter need to be understood in terms of values, a set of ethical principles that underpin practice. The central focus of the chapter is on the need to make our values explicit so that we can be clear about how they influence and shape our practice, and how compatible or otherwise they are with the professional values of social work.

Chapter 6 carries the title of 'Achieving good practice', and consists of a number of discussions around the steps that need to be taken to develop high standards of practice. There are no simple or clear-cut formulas to follow, but there are guidelines and principles that can help meet the challenge of developing good practice.

Chapter 7 is the final chapter, and addresses the difficulties, challenges and dilemmas social workers face on a day-to-day basis. Social work is not an easy option. Indeed, it is a very challenging and demanding occupation, and so it is necessary to be realistic about what is involved, about the challenges that have to be faced. But, being realistic does not mean being pessimistic or defeatist. Indeed, I shall be arguing that defeatism and cynicism are barriers to good practice. Being realistic, by contrast, lays the foundations for a positive and constructive approach to social work practice and the challenges it brings.

1

Making sense of social work

Introduction

The main focus of this chapter is the attempt to clarify the nature and purposes of social work – that is, to try to establish some degree of clarity about what social work is. As we shall see below, many people have offered definitions of social work, often with confusing results. The approach I shall adopt here, then, is to work towards an understanding of what social work is, rather than *begin* with a definition.

I shall approach the question of what social work is by looking at, first, how it differs from other occupations and disciplines and then what it has in common with many of them. This will set the scene for a discussion of what social work is and why its nature is so often misunderstood. Following on from this, I shall present my own view of social work and outline what I see as some of the basic building blocks of good practice.

Differences

Some people use the term 'social work' to refer to any type of activity that is geared towards helping people solve their problems. For example, during my own career as a social work practitioner, I was told by teachers, nurses and others that they too did 'social work'. In making such comments they were using a very broad definition of social work and, in so doing, failing to recognize some of the more specific aspects of the social work role, and some of the key differences between social work in particular and the helping professions in general. My task here, then, is to outline what some of those main differences are so that we can begin to build up a picture of what is distinctive about social work.

Statutory duties

Although all members of the human services, and indeed all occupational groups, are subject to the law, social workers have specific statutory duties that set them apart from other groups, as we shall explore in more detail in Chapter 2. These legal duties include, but are not limited to:

- investigating allegations of child abuse;
- applying, where necessary and appropriate, for a person to be detained in hospital when his or her mental condition presents a serious risk of harm to self or others; and
- supervising children in the care of the local authority.

Such duties are complex and often require consultation with legal specialists. These duties can also have a bearing on other professionals, but the point remains that they are *social work* duties.

Because of these statutory duties, social workers are legally accountable – they are answerable, under the law, for their actions or, in some cases, their inaction. In some instances, the ultimate responsibility lies with the local authority, rather than the individual social worker who acts as a representative of the authority. However, in other cases, as in the case of duties under the Mental Health Act 1983, it is the individual social worker who carries personal responsibility. This means that, where negligence is alleged, it is the individual social worker who would be held to account in law, and may therefore be the subject of a legal action.

Regardless of whether it is the individual or the employing organization that carries ultimate responsibility, the social worker is, of course, always accountable, morally and professionally, for his or her actions. It is for this reason that social workers should:

- be aware of what their legal duties are, and be prepared to carry them out to the best of their abilities;
- ensure that the necessary steps are taken to comply with the law, or where this is not possible for some reason, make this known formally to a senior member of staff;

- receive appropriate training, support and supervision in order to feel equipped to undertake their duties.

It is not surprising, perhaps, that many social work students comment in the early stages of their first practice placement that they had not realized just how closely linked social work practice is to the legal context. This is also something that members of other professions often do not appreciate. For example, a health visitor concerned about the welfare of a young child may wonder why the social worker concerned does not remove the child and place him or her with foster carers. The health visitor may not understand that the social worker is not free to act independently of the law, and that fairly strict criteria would have to be met and accepted by a court of law (or by a magistrate in an emergency outside the hours in which the courts operate). This can lead to tensions between workers, and so we should perhaps add to our list that social workers should, where necessary, make sure that other professionals involved in a particular case understand the statutory duties of the social worker, so that there is some degree of clarity about what can or cannot be done.

Care vs. control

Social work is, of course, one of the 'caring' or 'helping' professions, and so caring and helping are very much to the fore. However, it would be naïve not to recognize that there are also significant elements of social control. This is because social work involves promoting and protecting the welfare of not only the individual but also the wider community, a dual responsibility that can often lead to conflicts and tensions (see 'caught in the middle' below). Protecting the wider community is an example of *caring,* but, in relation to specific individuals, the same actions can amount to *control.*

This is not to say that other professional groups are not involved in matters of control, as clearly they are (for example, doctors are involved in detaining certain people in hospital against their will). The difference is that, for other groups of staff, control issues are generally marginal to the central purpose of their work. For social work, however, control issues can often be just as central as those of caring. Indeed, the two can be so intertwined that it is difficult to tell them apart. Examples of this 'intertwining' of care and control include:

- child protection;
- probation and youth justice work;
- dealing with elder abuse and the abuse of other vulnerable adults;
- compulsory admission to hospital in circumstances where a person's mental condition warrants this.

In this respect, control can be seen to be part of care. However, we should also recognize that control can, at times, become an end in itself, leaving little or no room for care. In such cases, practice can become oppressive, an additional problem for the client to deal with. For example, in working with someone with mental health problems, a social worker over-concerned with control issues may become pre-occupied with matters of 'policing' at the expense of meeting needs. Ironically, a failure to address the client's needs is likely to make for a more stressful situation, and therefore to make the need for policing even greater. The balance between care and control is therefore an important one for social workers to bear in mind – although it is often a difficult one to maintain. To ignore control is to run the risk of being ineffective (for example, by not fulfilling statutory duties and/or leaving vulnerable people unprotected), while to ignore care is likely to be not only ineffective but also potentially abusive and oppressive.

What has to be recognized is that social workers are in positions of power, and that power can be used positively and constructively to help people gain greater control over their lives (a process of *empowerment* – Braye and Preston-Shoot, 1995; Fook, 2002), or it can be used inappropriately and destructively in the form of abuse, exploitation and/or the reinforcement of existing disadvantages and inequalities (Thompson, 2003a). This theme of power, and its potential to go either way – empowerment or oppression – will be a recurring theme of this book, but it is particularly relevant to the question of managing the tension between care and control. Indeed, managing this tension can be seen as an exercise in the appropriate use of professional power.

Being 'caught in the middle'

One of the difficulties and demands of social work is that of being 'caught in the middle'. We have already seen that social work occupies the territory where care and control meet. But social work is also 'caught in the middle' between various other conflicting forces, not least between the individual and society. Clarke (1993) makes an important comment about this:

> Social workers have always been expected to balance the claims of the client's needs with the needs of society. To some extent, this balance has been resolved by assuming that the client's needs and society's needs are not in tension: restoring the client to 'normal functioning' satisfies everyone's interests. At other times, social workers have been less willing to accept this assumption of harmonious interests and have tried to redefine their role as the champions or advocates of the client. In other circumstances, social workers have insisted that, although clients may think they know what their needs are, social workers as society's expert representatives know better. (p. 19)

It is, of course, no coincidence that social workers find themselves 'caught in the middle'. This situation owes a great deal to the fact that social work is located at the intersection of 'personal troubles' and 'public ills' (Mills, 1959). That is, many of the problems individual clients encounter are closely linked to wider social concerns or problems in society, such as:

- poverty and deprivation;
- racism and other forms of social exclusion;
- inadequacies in housing, health care and education;
- crime and social unrest; and
- abuse and exploitation.

It can often be difficult for social workers to manage the conflicts inherent in being 'caught in the middle'. What can also make this more difficult is a lack of understanding of such conflicts on the part of others. This can lead to situations where social workers are criticized for not tackling a problem in a simple or direct way. A clear example of this arises in relation to child protection. In cases where children are suspected of being in need of protection from abuse, the social worker has to balance the need to ensure the child's safety against the danger of breaking up families unnecessarily through over-intrusive interventions. Someone who does not appreciate the sensitivities of such matters may easily dismiss the careful actions of the social worker as 'pussyfooting'. This is not to say that such a criticism is never applicable, but there is a very real danger that a lack of awareness of the 'caught in the middle' dilemma will lead to a great deal of unfair criticism – and possibly significant barriers to multidisciplinary collaboration as a result of the tensions and recriminations that can arise.

This dilemma is also one of the reasons why social workers cannot rely on simple, formula answers. Each situation has to be dealt with on its own merits, carefully analysed (assessment), with clear steps identified to address the situation (intervention) – a process of sensitive and well-informed professional practice, rather than the application of general rules in a uniform way. Formula responses do not equip social workers for dealing with the complexities of being 'caught in the middle'.

Doing society's 'dirty work'

One way of looking at social work is to see it as a 'sweeping up' operation, clearing up the problems caused by the failures or gaps in other social policies or systems. That is, social workers are asked to step in where 'society' has failed its citizens in some respect. Examples would include:

- elder abuse as a failure of a civilized society to treat its older citizens with dignity;
- crime as a failure of the education system and the moral order more generally, as well as a failure of the employment and welfare benefits systems;
- fostering and/or residential care of children as a failure of child welfare systems more broadly.

In this regard, social work can be seen as the 'patch up' system of the welfare state. In some respects, this is too narrow a view of social work, and it certainly does not capture the whole range of social work activities. However, there is, I would argue, at least a grain of truth in the argument, and it is certainly the case that social workers do at times feel as though they are charged with 'doing society's dirty work'. This is particularly so in relation to some aspects of practice where many members of the general public would prefer not to be reminded that such problems exist: child abuse, 'domestic' violence, terminal illness and so on.

In addition, where many people have a judgemental attitude towards recipients of social work help, viewing them as 'scroungers' or 'inadequates', such a negative judgement can also be applied to social workers, who are then stereotyped as naïve 'do-gooders', easily exploited by unscrupulous, streetwise clients. Although these views bear little resemblance to the realities of social work practice, we none the less have to recognize that it is not uncommon for people to hold such views.

Consequently, the general view of social work and social workers can be very mixed, partly very positive, but often also very negative – even where there may be no grounds for such negativity. The standing of social work is therefore mixed as a result of its 'structural location' – that is, the part it plays in society generally in relation to its problems or 'dirty work'. This is often illustrated by attitudes towards social workers in the media, particularly in national newspapers. Aldridge (1994) provides many examples of the ways in which the actions of social workers are often portrayed in unduly negative terms, particularly where child abuse cases are being reported. These can be seen as examples of situations where social workers are being used as scapegoats, blamed as individuals for problems that have more to do with wider structures and systems (Parton, 1985). Again, this is not to say that social workers never make mistakes, but there is clearly a world of difference between making a mistake on the one hand, and being blamed for matters beyond one's control on the other.

Although other professional groups do not escape criticism, these rarely, if ever, reach the proportions of the negative feelings that can be shown towards social work and the 'dirty work' that social workers do. This is therefore something that sets social work apart from other helping professions (the negative views of social work are discussed further in Chapter 7).

Working towards social justice

I mentioned earlier that social work is a *contested* entity, open to various interpretations. The question of 'working towards social justice' is a good example of this. Some of the more traditional conceptions of social work would focus narrowly on the individual and his or her family and would not concern themselves with broader questions of social justice (Halmos, 1965). Other conceptions, and certainly my own, would see a commitment to social justice as a central theme and defining feature of social work. For example, Preston-Shoot (1996) emphasizes the importance of promoting social justice and challenging oppression:

> If social work in particular, and professional groups with which it interacts, lose the ability or willingness to question, they risk losing the empathy, values and practice skills which seek to counter the inequalities, internalised oppression, alienation and exclusion characteristic of contemporary social life. They risk identifying with the aggressor rather than using their position to promote an empowering difference. (p. 39)

This willingness to question is part of a *critical* perspective on society and social problems that is, or should be, a fundamental part of social work. As we have seen, social work operates at the intersection of personal circumstances and broader social forces. Consequently, if practitioners do not adopt a questioning, critical perspective, there is a very worrying danger that they may reinforce existing inequalities, consolidating relatively powerless people in their powerlessness.

Because of this key position at the meeting point of the personal and the social (or, to be more precise, the *sociopolitical*), there can be no neutral middle ground – intervention will either challenge inequalities or reinforce them (Thompson, 2001). For example, in working with a black family or individual, a failure to recognize the significance of racism in their lives may well exacerbate tensions and reinforce feelings that black people's needs and experiences are not important in a white society. Similarly, Robinson (1995) argues that the application of psychological theories based on white norms to the circumstances of black people serves to devalue black experiences, values and lifestyles, to treat them as inferior to, or deviant from, their white equivalents.

By contrast, a social work practice which recognizes inequalities and power differentials between workers and clients has the potential to work positively towards *empowerment* through the promotion of equality and social justice. (This theme of empowerment is one which will recur in this and later chapters.)

Of course, issues of equality and social justice are not irrelevant to other human services. For example, inequality in health is a very significant issue for nurses and other health care professionals. However, my point is that, for social work, these issues are central to the enterprise, a defining feature of the nature and purpose of social work as an occupation. It is difficult to conceive of social work as a humanitarian endeavour unless we incorporate a commitment to taking whatever steps are possible towards eradicating the inequalities and injustices that are part and parcel of the social problems social workers seek to address.

Although the 'differences' outlined here are not necessarily exhaustive, they should be sufficient to make the point that social work is a distinctive professional activity, linked to, but different from, the other human services. Before moving on to consider the other side of the coin – the similarities – it is worth pausing to summarize the differences.

Social work can be seen as distinctive in terms of:

- the central role of statutory duties;
- the challenge of managing the tensions between care and control;
- the dilemmas of being 'caught in the middle';
- the need to do society's 'dirty work'; and
- the primacy of a commitment to social justice.

Commonalities

Social work is one discipline or profession amongst many that are concerned with the health and well-being of the populace or at least certain groups within the populace – for example, nurses and other health care workers; youth and community workers; housing officers; counsellors; advice workers; pastors and chaplains. It is not surprising, then, that social work has much in common with these groups. This section briefly reviews what those common themes are.

Humanitarianism

A humanitarian or compassionate approach is, of course, a fundamental component. However, there are conflicts and tensions between a personal commitment to humanitarian goals and one's status as a paid employee of an organization, quite often a large, bureaucratic organization. One of the possible consequences of this is for staff to become 'functionaries', to lose their compassion in a web of bureaucratic routines, procedures and standard practices.

One challenge, then, that applies across these professional groups is that of maintaining a compassionate and humanitarian approach in the face of pressures to conform to organizational expectations and interests which may not always be compatible with the interests of the individual or family concerned, or with the values of the profession. Supervision can and should be of value in this respect (Morrison, 2000), but each individual worker also has a responsibility to do whatever he or she can to avoid falling into the tramlines of routine, uncritical practice that has lost its heart (see the discussion of 'burnout' in Chapter 7).

A professional knowledge base

As we shall see in more detail in Chapter 3, social workers need to draw on an extensive knowledge base in order to be equipped to meet the challenges of the work. This is something that is shared with other professional groups, with some of the knowledge being shared across such groups (knowledge of how communication works, for example), while some aspects are more specific to particular groups (for example, anatomy for health care professionals).

Sometimes the breadth and depth of the knowledge base of the caring professions is not appreciated, particularly by members of the general public. This is perhaps partly due to assumptions about caring tasks being 'common sense' and requiring little or no specialist knowledge or skills. It is perhaps also due to assumptions about gender and employment – skilled, professional work being associated with men (and the predominantly male professions of law, medicine and so on), while the less skilled, more 'practical' work is more closely associated with women (and the predominantly female caring professions).

Whatever assumptions may be made about the knowledge base of the helping professions in general and social work in particular, the fact remains that good practice depends on the appropriate use of an extensive knowledge base.

A set of skills

Arguably, knowledge on its own is of little use if it cannot be put into practice, and so a basic set of skills needed by all practitioners is that of being able to utilize knowledge appropriately – that is, to integrate theory and practice. However, there are also many other skills involved, and it is once again a case of going beyond common-sense notions that work in the caring professions is relatively straightforward and unskilled. As we shall see in Chapter 4, the skills involved in social work are many and varied, and often need to be developed to quite advanced levels.

Many of the skills involved are not restricted to the helping professions. Indeed, many of the 'people skills' apply to a whole host of occupations that bring staff into contact with other people in order to solve a particular problem or address a particular set of issues: communication, planning, assertiveness and so on. Furthermore, many of the skills – being able to 'read' non-verbal communication, for example – are part and parcel of the social skills necessary for everyday life. However, an important point to emphasize here is that it is necessary to *develop* such skills, to raise them beyond the everyday level. Indeed, a lot of emphasis in professional training is placed on the enhancement of existing skills.

A value base

Although values can be very personal and individualistic, they can also be shared by a group of people with common aims, as in the case of members of a particular profession. Social work is a good example of this, with values playing a major part in education and training, policy making and the professional literature base in general.

As we shall see in Chapter 5, social work has a distinctive value base, although this is not to say that it has nothing in common with other professions. Of course, there is a significant degree of overlap, albeit with many differences of emphasis and interpretation.

Values are sets of beliefs and principles that have an important role to play in terms of:

- providing a guide to action;
- offering a framework for making sense of practice;
- providing a yardstick by which to judge the appropriateness or otherwise of particular actions;
- generating a degree of motivation and commitment.

One of the significant features of values is that we tend to become so accustomed to our own values and beliefs that we do not recognize that they are there or how they are influencing us. An important step, then, is to be clear about what our values are.

Professional discretion and accountability

As we have seen, professional practice involves not only knowledge and skills, but also values. As Jordan (1990) comments: 'moral reasoning is not an alternative to knowledge of the law and social policy, but it is an essential addition to them' (p. 3). He links this to professional discretion and goes on to argue that:

> The law provides the framework of rules under which social workers operate; policy provides an interpretation of those rules, and a commentary on their purposes. But there would be no point in using social workers to do these tasks if laws and policies could be precisely and unambiguously stated; it is because situations are complex and susceptible to a number of interpretations that the judgement, discretion and skill of a trained person are required. As Harris and Webb [1987] have remarked, 'professionals do not create discretion; rather the inevitability of discretion creates the need for professionals'. But what

needs to be interpreted, discussed, negotiated and communicated has an inescapable moral content. (pp. 3–4)

Social workers, like others in the human services, have to exercise professional discretion. That is, the nature of the work is such that judgements have to be made about how to proceed, and such judgements:

- inevitably involve values – they are not made in an ethical 'vacuum';
- have consequences, good or bad, and therefore involve risk;
- make the worker accountable for his or her actions.

As we shall see in Chapter 5, making professional judgements is not the same as being judgemental. However, the need to make judgements (discretion) is everpresent, in so far as 'people work' involves so many variations, complications and uncertainties that simple, formula responses are not appropriate. Both discretion and accountability are therefore fundamental aspects of practice. This is a point that has been recognized in the National Occupational Standards which make reference to the importance of professional accountability.

As with the list of differences outlined earlier, the commonalities identified here are by no means the only ones, but should none the less be sufficient to provide an overview of some of the important interconnections between social work and the other helping professions.

To summarize, then, social work 'shares' with other professional groups in the human services:

- a humanitarian or compassionate approach;
- a professional knowledge base;
- a set of skills;
- practice based on values;
- discretion and accountability.

What is social work?

The discussions so far in this chapter have paved the way for addressing the fundamental question of: 'What is social work?' Of course, there is no single, simple answer to this question. Social work is a political entity and so, of course, how it is defined, conceptualized and implemented is therefore a contested matter. Readers looking for a simple, non-controversial answer should therefore prepare to be disappointed!

One definition which has been put forward is that of the International Association of Schools of Social Work and the International Federation of Social Workers:

> a profession which promotes social change, problem solving in human relationships and the empowerment and liberation of people to enhance well-being. Utilising theories of human behaviour and social systems, social work intervenes at the points where people interact with their environments. Principles of human rights and social justice are fundamental to social work. (2001, cited in NISCC, 2003)

I find this a helpful definition as it incorporates many of the elements of the preceding discussions, but even this leaves scope for debate and dissent. However, we have to be careful not to get bogged down in finding *the* definition of social work and losing sight of its variability, its complexity and its status as a contested entity.

How particular writers or organizations define social work will depend, to a large extent, on their view of what social work should be. For example, Payne (1997) describes three different approaches to social work. These are:

- *Individualism-reformism*   This refers to a view of social work as an activity geared towards meeting social welfare needs on an individualized basis.
- *Socialist-collectivist*   For Payne, this approach 'is part of a system which seeks to promote co-operation in society so that the most oppressed and disadvantaged people can gain power over their own lives' (1997, p. 2).
- *Reflexive-therapeutic*   This approach is geared towards promoting and facilitating personal growth in order to enable people to deal with the suffering and disadvantage they experience.

Adherents of these approaches will define social work in terms of their view of what social work should be. Different approaches will produce different definitions. And, of course, the types described by Payne are 'pure' types – there also exist various combinations of elements from across the three.

In view of these complexities I shall avoid the rather fruitless task of coming up with a single definition of social work. Instead, I shall explore some important issues that should help provide an understanding of what social work is, without necessarily producing a clear and explicit definition. What follows, then, is an account of some key issues relating to the nature and purpose of social work.

Social work is what social workers do

At one level, we could simply say that social work is what social workers do. That is, we could take a descriptive approach and list the sorts of activities that social work involves:

- assessing the needs and circumstances of those who request, or who are referred for, social work help;
- purchasing/commissioning and/or providing services to meet identified needs, or ameliorate a harmful or unsatisfactory situation;
- engaging in problem-solving, facilitative and supportive activities at the level of the individual, the family, group or community;
- assessing the degree and nature of risk to which vulnerable individuals are exposed;
- establishing, implementing and evaluating protection plans;
- providing reports for courts in order to assist in determining the most appropriate outcome;
- contributing to multidisciplinary schemes and projects to support, and benefit from, the efforts of other professionals;
- providing or arranging advocacy or mediation;
- working with community groups, individuals and families to address social problems on a preventative basis;
- undertaking statutory duties in accordance with a number of Acts of Parliament.

However, while this may be helpful in providing a picture of the range of activities that come under the umbrella of 'social work', it still does not really answer the question. It is also quite vague as a result of the level of generality. Furthermore, it involves a significant degree of overlap with descriptions of other human services.

An additional weakness of this approach, of course, is that it is incomplete. It will always be possible for someone else to come along and add another item to the list!

Social work vs. social welfare

Another way of addressing the question of 'What is social work?' is to locate social work in its broader context as part of the wider concept of social welfare. As Skidmore *et al.* (1997) comment:

The terms *social work* and *social welfare* are often confused and sometimes used synonymously. Actually, social welfare has a broader meaning and encompasses social work, public welfare and other related programs and activities. Social welfare, according to Friedlander, 'is the organized system of social services and institutions, designed to aid individuals and groups to attain satisfying standards of life and health, and personal and social relationships that permit them to develop their full capacities and to promote their well being in harmony with the needs of their families and the community'. (p. 3)

Social work can therefore be seen as one form of social welfare amongst others, alongside youth and community work, housing welfare, advice work and so on.

A related approach is to present social work in terms of 'the personal social services'. This relates to the area of social policy that is concerned with the welfare of particular individuals or groups, rather than with the populace generally (as in the case of health and education, for example). This is significant in terms of the tension between the needs of the individual and those of the broader society (personal vs. social). This manifests itself in the following ways:

- Social work operates at the intersection of the personal and the social (a point to which we shall return below).
- The recipients of social work services are often stigmatized and disadvantaged.
- The role of the personal social services is to seek to redress the inequalities such people experience.
- Social work, although geared towards addressing social inequalities and related problems, functions at the level of individual and group needs and problems, rather than through social activism.

The conceptualization of social work as the central plank of the personal social services (and one part of the broader field of social welfare) still does not provide a definitive statement of what social work is. However, it does take us further forward in developing our understanding, and it also raises important issues that will feature in further discussions below.

History and purpose

A further possibility for arriving at a definition of social work is to consider:

1. What is the history of social work? How did it arise?
2. What is the purpose of social work? Why does it exist?

While a detailed and thorough analysis of the historical roots of social work could help broaden and deepen our appreciation, it would still not give us a definitive statement. This is because social work is a fluid entity – it grows, develops and changes. Consequently, we cannot necessarily define present (or future) social work by reference to past work. By contrast, considering the *purpose* of social work could prove far more fruitful.

I made the point earlier that social work is a contested concept, with different perspectives on what it is and how it should be practised. Similarly, the question of what social work is *for* is one that is highly contested. Indeed, there are many schools of thought about the nature and purpose of social work (and social welfare more broadly), and many authors have developed typologies or classification systems to distinguish between the different approaches (Forder *et al.,* 1984; George and Wilding, 1994). It is certainly beyond the scope of this book to explore the complexities of the various approaches and typologies. I shall therefore limit myself to one theme to emerge from a consideration of these issues, namely the distinction between conceptions of social work as an agency of social stability and an agency of social change. In some ways, this is an oversimplification of a highly complex situation, but it can none the less be helpful as an introduction to the intricacies of the debate about what social work is for.

Social work and social stability

It can be argued that the role of social work is to contribute to social stability, to ensure that the level of social discontent does not reach a point where the social order may be threatened. A generous reading of this role is that it is geared towards enabling disadvantaged members of society to function effectively in society – it is a *caring* response. By contrast, a more sceptical perspective on this role is that it is geared towards protecting the status quo of power and privilege from the threat of a disenfranchised 'underclass' – it is a *controlling* response. Many traditional approaches to social work are premised on this notion of social stability. The primary task, it would seem, is to help people adjust to their social circumstances and learn how to function better within them. The possibility of changing those social circumstances is afforded only secondary consideration, if at all.

One key assumption underpinning this approach is what can be called a 'consensus' model of society (Thompson, 1992a). That is, it is assumed that society as a whole has the same basic interests and goals – that there is a consensus of moral and political values. According to this view of society, the task of social work is to help deal with personal and social problems at a personal or interpersonal level so that people can overcome, or adjust to, any personal difficulties that may be preventing them from sharing in the common good.

Consensus-based approaches are closely associated with a 'medical' model of social work. Here, the social worker is seen as a form of 'doctor' who diagnoses what is wrong with an individual or family, and prescribes a programme of treatment. This was, at one time, a dominant model of social work practice. It is only relatively recently that the term 'diagnosis' has been dropped from the social work vocabulary, and the term 'treatment' is still widely used, especially in a child protection context. According to this model:

- The social worker is the expert and therefore occupies a very powerful position.
- Although social circumstances are relevant, the primary problem (or 'pathology') is seen to lie in the individual or in the family.
- A successful outcome is either a 'cure' for the problem or an alleviation of the 'symptoms' so that a return to 'healthy' society can be facilitated.

Social work and social change

The consensus approach can be seen to be seriously flawed in so far as it neglects the inherent tensions and divisions in society (Thompson, 2001). An alternative perspective is to see social work as part of a process of social change and amelioration. This approach is premised on a view of society characterized not by moral and political consensus with common interests, but rather by significant social divisions and conflicts of interest. These social divisions include class, race and gender, along with many others.

According to this view, the recipients of social work help are predominantly members of oppressed minorities whose problems owe more to the structure of society than to their own personal failings or inadequacies. The task of social work, then, is to support oppressed individuals, groups and communities in challenging the discrimination and inequality to which they are routinely and systematically exposed.

This is an approach that is closely associated with what became known as 'radical social work', a perspective that emphasized the importance of working towards social change, rather than simply helping people adjust to their disadvantaged position.

According to this model:

- Society is characterized more by conflict and division than by consensus.
- The task is not to return people to a 'healthy' society, but rather to work towards promoting social change by supporting oppressed minorities in their struggle against discrimination and inequality.
- Social work is not a morally or politically neutral exercise in technical problem solving, but rather a set of activities geared towards promoting equality and social justice.

Social stability and social change

As far as the consensus and conflict models are concerned, it will be clear from the chapters that follow that I have little sympathy with the former and mixed feelings about the latter. As I have argued elsewhere (Thompson, 2003a), a medical model approach to social work is highly problematic. It reduces complex social and interpersonal problems to matters of individual failing or 'dysfunction'. The radical school of thought succeeds in locating social work in its sociopolitical context and highlights the importance of power and inequality in the development of social problems and as a barrier to addressing them. However, at least some forms of radical social work appear to make a number of fundamental errors in their analysis of the relationship between social work, the state and the wider society:

- Social work practice is rooted in law and policy. While it can challenge or work against these factors to a certain degree, it cannot transcend them altogether.
- By and large, social workers are paid employees, often of statutory agencies. Their actions are therefore constrained by the policies, values and aims of their employing organizations (if they wish to continue as employees).
- Although structural factors are clearly important aspects of the development of social problems, these interrelate with cultural and personal factors (Thompson, 2001). An unbalanced emphasis on structural factors can leave social workers feeling powerless and helpless.

What I wish to propose here, then, is an approach that builds on the strengths of the consensus and conflict approaches, but seeks to avoid their weaknesses. A consensus approach associates social work with social stability, while a conflict approach would concentrate on social change. However, I believe a more realistic view of social work is one that focuses on *both* social stability *and* social change.

In some ways, the approach I develop below could be seen as a form of radical social work. However, I would be using the term 'radical' in its literal sense to mean 'at the root'. The problems social workers seek to address are *social* problems, and therefore have their roots in society – in patterns of social relationships, distributions of power and resources, and attitudes and values. A radical approach is therefore one that seeks to address problems at a social level. However, to be realistic, it must be recognized that there are limits to how far this can go or how it can be done. It is important to avoid the naïve idealism associated with earlier forms of radical social work. As Davies (1991) comments:

> Whatever the arguments of those who saw in social work an unaccept-able vehicle for the oppression of the poor, the radical idea of using social workers as agents of political reform seemed to reveal – then as now – an astonishing naïvety about the sociology of organisations, the relative powerlessness of individuals within them, and the importance of self-interest as a motivating force in any occupational group. There was bound to be a bitter harvest of disillusionment. (p. 4)

This is not to say that social work cannot contribute to social change and amelioration. Indeed, I shall be arguing below that it most certainly can. However, optimism about achieving change must be combined with realism about the obstacles to be faced and the limits on likely success. We should also consider the question of timescales. While social changes may not be likely in the short term, this should not deter us from working towards changes in the longer term, a point to which I shall return below.

Working towards social change, however, does not mean that social stability is not important. Trying to make a contribution to developing a more humane, compassionate society in which discrimination and oppression are not tolerated does not preclude working to maintain and safeguard many aspects of the social order. Social work can, then, legitimately claim to contribute to social stability without reinforcing inequalities or social injustices. That is, social work can work towards

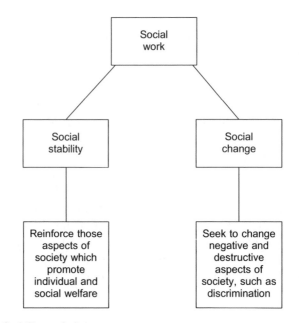

Figure 1.1 Stability and change

social change *and* social stability – it is an oversimplification to see the two as mutually exclusive.

This leaves us, though, with a crucial question: what aspects of society need to be changed, and what aspects are worthy of safeguarding? How we respond to this will depend, of course, on our values – on our view of the type of society we wish to be part of. It is partly for this reason that values merit a chapter of their own (Chapter 5).

Forging a new perspective

Webb (1996) argues that:

> What passes for social work is the product of the varying capacity of certain institutions and agencies to give it a particular definition to shape what it is that constitutes legitimate professional knowledge and the manner in which the delivery of services should be organised. (p. 173)

What counts as social work will depend on how powerful groups and institutions conceive of the social work role and tasks – it is a contested concept, contested in and through a process of shaping and reshaping, as competing groups and interests vie for dominance in putting their own stamp on the profession.

In view of this, my task here is to present what I see as the basis of social work practice, particularly of good practice. What follows, then, is not intended as 'the right answer', but rather my contribution to the debate about the nature and purpose of social work. It involves a rather complex philosophy, but one that has to be so to do justice to the complexities of the social work world it seeks to explain. If, in the following few pages, you find you are struggling to take on board the main points being presented, do not worry about this – it is difficult material to assimilate. You may prefer to come back to this section later after you have read some of the other chapters.

The existential basis of social work

My aim is not to present a detailed analysis of existentialist philosophy and its relevance to social work. Rather, I wish to point out the value of trying to understand social work in the context of some of the fundamental elements of human existence. I shall concentrate on four such aspects.

1. Ontology

Ontology is the study of being and is therefore concerned with questions about what it means to exist – the sorts of questions that are generally of little interest to us in our day-to-day lives, but which can take on major significance at times of loss or at turning points in our lives.

I see ontology as an important issue for social work because, as we have seen, social work operates at the intersection of the personal and the social. Human existence, ontologically speaking, is simultaneously personal *and* social. It is not a question of individual vs. society, but rather the individual *in* society (and, indeed, society in the individual, in the sense that social factors are a major influence in shaping the individual). Ontology teaches us that we should not see the personal and the social as entirely separate, but rather as interlocking aspects of human existence.

2. Existential challenges

Human existence presents us with a series of challenges to meet or problems to solve. These can be classified under three broad headings:

- *Life course challenges* These are the changes we encounter as we move through the life course: growing up, establishing independence, and so on, right through to facing up to death.

- *Challenges of circumstance* These are the challenges and problems that arise for specific individuals in specific circumstances – that is, the challenges we face as a result of the particular goals we are trying to achieve or lifestyle we are trying to live.
- *Sociopolitical challenges* These are the problems that can arise as a result of our position in society, our 'social location'. These include poverty, racism, sexism and other forms of exploitation.

No-one, of course, has a problem-free life, but it can be seen that problems are more likely at transition points in the life course (having children, divorce, retirement and so on) and are more likely (and probably more intense) for groups who are socially disadvantaged as a result of their social location. These problems can be referred to as existential challenges because they are part and parcel of human existence. They are inherent in being human, rather than incidental to it.

The notion of 'existential challenges' is an important one, as it is helpful in trying to understand the nature of social work. Indeed, it could be argued that much of social work practice involves helping people deal with existential challenges.

3. Uncertainty and flux

One of the key themes of existentialism is that of 'contingency'. This refers to the uncertain and ever-changing nature of human existence. Very few things in life are certain. However, for people experiencing the types of problems that bring them to social workers – and indeed for social workers themselves – uncertainty is often much to the fore. For example, when a case of child abuse comes to light, the child, the parents and the social worker all face a considerable degree of uncertainty (Thompson, 1992b). Trying to find simple answers can do more harm than good in many situations, and it is often not possible to relieve the uncertainty, not in the short to medium term at least. Consequently, a basic task for the social worker in very many situations is the *management* of uncertainty.

Similarly, both the problems that lead to social work intervention and the nature of social work intervention are characterized by change or '*flux*'. And, of course, uncertainty and change tend to reinforce each other. Any attempt, then, to find simple, formula answers is doomed to failure, as such an approach does not pay adequate attention to uncertainty and change. Social work responses have to be tailor made to suit the circumstances at the time and cannot be 'off the peg', once-and-for-all solutions.

As a result of uncertainty and *flux,* social work practice needs to be:

- *Systematic*   This means having a clear focus on what we are trying to achieve and why. This is important because uncertainty and change can easily lead to practice becoming vague and unfocused, and therefore ineffective.
- *Reflective* Unthinking, uncritical practice can be dangerous, especially where uncertainty and change are to the fore. It is therefore necessary for practice to be reflective – carefully thought through and reflected on, open to change and development where necessary.

Clearly, then, social work practice needs to be sensitive and responsive to uncertainty and *flux.*

4. Moral commitment

Another central theme of existentialism is that of *engagement* or 'moral commitment'. The basic argument is that we cannot be morally or politically neutral. Our actions will either support and reinforce the status quo (and the current distribution of power and life chances associated with it) or they will challenge it – there is no neutral ground in which our actions have no moral or political consequences.

This is a general principle, but it is particularly relevant to issues of inequality, discrimination and oppression. That is, given that we live in a society characterized by various forms of inequality, the actions and interactions of social workers will either reinforce (or at least condone) existing inequalities, or will play a part in challenging or undermining them (Thompson, 2001). This is a point to which I shall return in Chapter 5.

A social work practice that takes no account of existing inequalities runs the risk of:

- failing to recognize important factors in people's lives, and therefore basing intervention on very unsafe foundations;
- causing tension, ill-feeling and resentment as a result of what can come across to clients as an uncaring, insensitive approach;
- reinforcing the negative effects of discrimination; for example, adopting a paternalistic, patronizing attitude towards an older person is likely to reinforce the ageist assumption that older people are 'past it', and not of value to society.

Social work operates, then, not only at the intersection of the personal and the social, but also at the intersection of competing forces seeking to influence and shape society. There is a fundamental moral question of which set of forces our practice will support. As the forces geared towards retaining the status quo tend to be dominant, a supposedly 'neutral' stance is, in effect, a vote for the status quo.

My argument here, then, is that social work should be:

- explicit about its value base;
- committed to demonstrating these values;
- clear that the notion of a value-free practice is a (potentially dangerous) myth;
- *emancipatory,* in the sense of being geared towards supporting people in their struggles to break free from the disadvantage, discrimination and oppression they experience as a result of their social location.

Summary

In sum, a social work practice premised on the principles of existentialism should be:

- *ontological* – sensitive to the personal and social dimensions and the interactions between the two;
- *problem focused* – sensitive and responsive to the existential challenges we all face, but particularly those that are related to social location and social divisions;
- *systematic* – with a clear focus on what we are doing and why (our goals and our plans for achieving them);
- *reflective* – open-minded, carefully thought-through and a source of constant learning rather than a rigid, routinized approach to practice;
- *emancipatory* – attuned to issues of inequality, discrimination and oppression, and geared towards countering them where possible.

Conclusion

The main focus of this chapter has been the development of an understanding of what social work is, a picture of what it involves. This was tackled in three ways. First, I outlined the differences between social work and the other helping professions or human services more broadly, and the commonalities across them. Second, I explored a number of attempts to define social work, but without getting bogged down in trying to pin down a precise definitive statement. Third, I argued that social work is 'up for grabs' in the sense that what constitutes social work depends on the outcome of attempts by powerful groups and institutions to shape social work policy and practice. On this basis, I then proposed my own 'submission' of how social work should be seen by relating it to some of the key themes of a particular school of philosophy, namely existentialism.

My aim has not been to close the debate or provide a once-and-for-all solution, as that would be both unhelpful and unrealistic. Rather, I have attempted to provide a picture of the complex reality of contemporary social work, together with some guidelines as to what I see as a useful and constructive way forward. In this regard, this chapter has provided a foundation for the chapters that follow, each of which should help to develop the beginnings of understanding presented here.

Guide to further learning

Stepney and Ford (2000) and Davies (2002) both provide a useful introduction to social work practice, while Payne (1997) provides a good overview of the various perspectives on the theory base underpinning social work (to be discussed in more detail in Chapter 3). Payne (1996) provides a helpful detailed exposition of the debate about what social work is. Thompson and Thompson (2002) is geared towards social care workers more broadly, but none the less contains some very relevant materials for social workers.

Hanvey and Philpot (1994) and Carter et al. (1995) both provide useful introductory material, as does Davies (1994), a classic text. Fook (2002) provides a very clear and helpful account of social work from a critical perspective. Parton (1996) is an interesting set of readings that explores some important issues. Brechin et al. (2000) is a thought-provoking set of essays, while May et al. (2001) is a useful starting point for understanding social problems.

As far as the existential basis of social work is concerned, Thompson (2000a) is a good starting point. Thompson (1992a) provides a thorough analysis, but is perhaps rather heavy going for people not used to academic social work texts. Thompson (1992b) is shorter and more accessible, but relates only to child protection, rather than to social work more broadly. Chapter 4 of Thompson (2000b) should also be helpful. I have presented my ideas of emancipatory practice in an introductory text (Thompson, 2001) and in a further book at a more advanced level (Thompson, 2003a).

Exercise 1

This exercise is designed to help you develop your own perspective on social work. Consider the following questions and use the space below to make some notes.

1. What is it about social work that interests you or appeals to you?
2. What do you think you have to offer to social work, and what rewards or benefits do you feel it offers you in return?
3. What sort of society do you think we would have if we did not have social work?
4. If you were a client, what would you expect from your social worker?

2

The legal and policy context

Introduction

Although it is clear that social workers have a considerable degree of professional autonomy in some respects, the steps that can be taken are heavily constrained by the law and the policies that arise from it. The law also lays down a number of duties – steps that social workers are obliged to take in certain circumstances. It is therefore essential that social workers have a good working knowledge of the law.

This is not to say that social workers need to have an in-depth knowledge of all of the legal provisions that apply to the various aspects of social work practice. However, it is necessary for practitioners to have at least a basic understanding of:

- the fundamental principles of law and the legislative process;
- the relationship between law and policy;
- the specific provisions of statutes that have a direct bearing on the particular area of practice in question;
- how and where to obtain further information and support when needed.

This chapter is intended as a starting point for the development of such understanding. It will not provide all that you need to know, but it will certainly offer a good start in the process of getting to grips with the complexities and intricacies of law and policy. It is a fairly 'packed' chapter, in the sense that it covers a great deal of material. You may therefore find it helpful to skim read it to begin with and then return to read it again more fully after you have read the other chapters.

Before looking at some of the key issues relating to the law and its relationship with social work, it is first necessary to consider where the law comes from, its status in relation to the state more broadly. I therefore begin by looking at the basic building blocks of the British Constitution.

The Constitution

The term 'Constitution' refers to the way in which the state of a particular nation and its authority are formally constituted. Unlike many other countries, Britain does not have a written Constitution. There are, of course, many written documents that contribute to the Constitution, such as Acts of Parliament that relate to the con-stitutional machinery (relating to voting rights and procedures, for example). And, of course, there are important historical documents, such as the *Magna Carta,* that also form part of the Constitution. However, there is no unifying or consolidating document or set of documents that form the basis of a written Constitution.

Of course, we should not make the mistake of assuming that the absence of a written constitution can be equated with the absence of a constitution *per se*. It is not the case that 'anything goes'. The authority and procedures of the state are firmly established, both in history and in the everyday practice of government.

An important element of the Constitution is convention. That is, many aspects of constitutional practice derive from conventions estab-lished through custom and practice. For example, the impartiality of the Speaker of the House of Commons is something that has evolved over a period of time – it is not something that is formally recorded in statute or any other official document or written agreement.

Despite its flexibility and largely unwritten nature, the Constitution is none the less an extremely important and powerful foundation of the legal and policy context in which social work operates, and in which the whole of the state machinery and public life more generally operate. It is for this reason that we need to have an understanding of some of the key elements of the Constitution in order to understand the foundations of social work law and policy. I shall begin by exploring the three 'arms' of the state and their role in keeping the constitutional wheels turning: the legislature, the judiciary and the executive.

The legislature

The term 'legislature' is used to refer to that part of the state that is responsible for producing, amending and discontinuing the specific pieces of legislation that form the basis of the country's legal context. I shall have more to say below about the process from which new laws emerge, but I shall confine myself for present purposes to a brief discussion of *who* is involved in producing the body of law.

Primary responsibility for legislation lies with Parliament, the sum total of elected Members of Parliament (MPs) and, in the UK case at least, members of the House of Lords. The 'driving force' for particular pieces of legislation is generally the 'cabinet', a group consisting of the most senior members of the Government (that is, the most senior members of the majority party). However, individual MPs can also be the source of specific Acts of Parliament, known as Private Members' Bills. However, these form only a very small proportion of the legal base overall.

The judiciary

Once laws have been passed, steps have to be taken to ensure that breaches of the law are dealt with and that disputes arising from the law are resolved. That is, *a judicial* system has to be in place, a system of courts in which the relevant judgements can be made. The term 'judiciary' refers to those people charged with administering this system.

There are basically two types of major player in the judicial system – judges and magistrates – but with a lot of supporting characters, such as clerks, solicitors, barristers and so on. Although judges and magistrates play a broadly similar role in many ways, there are also significant differences. Judges are professionally trained, highly experienced lawyers who have 'worked their way up the ranks'. They have considerably more power than magistrates and operate at the higher court levels.

Magistrates, by contrast, are not professional lawyers. They are lay representatives of the community and receive expenses rather than a salary (although there does exist a small number of 'stipendiary' magistrates who receive a salary). Magistrates clearly need to have some degree of understanding of the law, although their primary role is to represent the community, and society more broadly, rather than provide legal expertise.

Magistrates who operate in the youth courts receive special training in dealing with matters relating to children and young people, although this is not intended to be sufficient to make them into child care experts.

Magistrates are principally concerned with matters relating to lawbreaking, and so it is mainly the judges who are involved in the matters that have most bearing on the development of law and policy. This can be seen to apply in three main ways by:

- dealing with breaches of the law, particularly in relation to more serious or more complex cases, and those that involve organizations, rather than individuals;
- adjudicating on disputes or controversies arising from the law, clarifying the way forward in those grey areas of the legal base that are not clear cut and therefore require some degree of interpretation;
- the process of 'judicial review' whereby individuals or organizations can apply to the courts to challenge a decision made, for example, by a local authority.

In each of these three cases the judiciary can not only implement or uphold the law, but also create further law through the process of *precedent setting,* a point to which I shall return below.

The executive

This is a term which refers to the branch of the state that is charged with implementing the elements of law and policy. It consists of various groups of people, the two major sets being the civil service and the officers of local authorities.

The civil service is divided into different departments and agencies, each of which is answerable to a senior MP or 'Minister'. In principle, then, the legislature makes policy while civil servants actually implement it. As Alcock (1996) comments:

> In theory then, policy is decided by the cabinet in *Westminster*, and is implemented by the civil servants in *Whitehall*. This Westminster-Whitehall division symbolizes the split between the democratic (policy making) aspect of the state, and the bureaucratic (policy implementation) aspect of it. Although, as books that concentrate in more detail on the policy-making and policy-implementation reveal, this division is far from a watertight one in practice – many MPs play little part in policy making and some civil servants have much power and influence over it (Ham and Hill, 1993). (p. 50)

There is a strong parallel between what happens in central government and the workings of local government. While central government has MPs and civil servants, local government has local councillors (elected members) and local authority officers. The parallel also applies in terms of the relationship between the two respective groups. That is, while councillors carry primary responsibility for policy making, it is clear that senior officers also play a major role. For example, the Director of Social Services and his or her senior colleagues are likely to play a key role in shaping policy.

The relationship between central and local government is also an important feature of the executive. The general principle is that matters of national concern are dealt with at a central government level, while those that relate more specifically to particular areas or regions are dealt with at a local level. Consequently, one of the roles of local government is to interpret and adapt national policies and guidelines to suit the local circumstances. For example, while the NHS and Community Care Act 1990 applies across the whole of Britain, each local authority is charged with developing its own Community Care Plan in which more detailed proposals for implementing community care policy are to be found.

However, in recent years the traditional relationship between central and local government has changed quite markedly. The Conservative Government in office between 1979 and 1997 took a number of steps to curb the powers of local government and to strengthen the position of central government. During that time, then, the shaping of policy became more and more a matter for central government.

These, then, are the three main components of the state, as currently constituted: the legislature, the judiciary and the executive. This is not to say that they are the only key players in the development and implementation of the legal and policy context. Pressure groups are

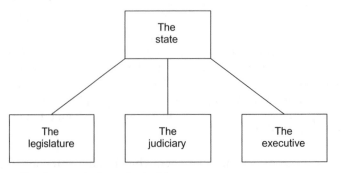

Figure 2.1 The three main 'branches' of the state

but one example of important elements in the process, and so we should be careful not to confuse *main* components with *sole* components. Indeed, it can be seen that pressure groups have played a major role in the development of many social policies and related pieces of legislation (for example, the influence of Shelter in developing policies relating to homelessness and the Child Poverty Action Group in relation to poverty and income maintenance).

Recent developments

The coming to power of the Labour Government in 1997 heralded a new era for the Constitution as a result of a commitment to devolution. Major changes occurred in 1999 as a result of this. A parliament specifically for Scotland was set up, with the capacity and authority to create, implement and administer new laws within certain limits, and to raise additional taxes if required. In Wales, a national assembly was established, with similar law-making powers, but without the power to raise additional taxes.

Since then, there has been the implementation, in October, 2000, of the Human Rights Act 1998, which has the effect of making the European Convention on Human Rights a part of the UK legal system. Proposals have also been put forward for the dissolution of the hereditary basis of the House of Lords.

These changes illustrate that, although the Constitution is relatively stable as a bedrock of UK society, it is none the less subject to change over time. Indeed, the whole of society is a gradually changing and developing process.

The process of law

In this section my aim is to provide a description of the process by which laws and related policies come into being, from initial point of concern to final working policy. In so doing, I will chart the key 'milestones' along the way.

Defining the problem

Laws and policies begin with the recognition of a problem or concern. Where it is felt by certain people (particularly people in positions of power) that a particular matter is a cause for concern and needs to be addressed, we could well be at the beginning of a long process that will culminate in the implementation of an Act of Parliament.

An important point to emphasize here is that *social problems are socially constructed* (Hulley and Clarke, 1991). That is, what constitutes a social problem depends on a range of social factors and priorities – what is seen as a problem in a particular society will owe a great deal to the values, structures and power relations of that society. For example, in a society where the absolute sanctity of marriage is highly valued, divorce may be seen as a social problem (and therefore probably prohibited or at least discouraged by law). By contrast, in a society where the sanctity of marriage is not given such a high priority, divorce may actually be seen as a solution to other problems, rather than a problem in its own right. In this way, identifying what a particular society defines as a social problem can tell us a lot about the society in question.

This means that problems will often be *contested* – subject to different interpretations and perspectives. Indeed, the contested nature of social work, as discussed in Chapter 1, owes much to contested definitions of social problems, in so far as social work can be seen as a response to social problems. If we disagree about what is a problem and what is not, it is not surprising that there should be disagreement about how we organize our responses to those problems.

Researching the problem

Once it has been recognized that there is a problem or set of concerns to be addressed, a common next step is for the Government to set up a working party of some description (by appointing a Royal Commission, for example) in order to explore the issues in some depth and consider some possible measures to tackle the concerns identified.

Such a working party would generally invite submissions from interested parties such as professional associations, recognized experts, user groups and so on. On the basis of this 'evidence', a detailed report would be compiled, summarizing the key issues and presenting a set of recommendations as to how the concerns identified should be addressed.

In most cases, the report produced will form the basis of subsequent legislation, although the government of the day is, of course, under no obligation to accept the recommendations or even the substance of the report. An example of this process would be the Griffiths Report (so called because the committee investigating the issues was chaired by Sir Roy Griffiths). This report (Griffiths, 1988) formed the basis of the NHS and Community Care Act 1990, although the Government did not adopt all of the recommendations.

Although this process has lain behind the development of many pieces of social policy, it is often bypassed, with the Government proposing legislation without such a formal process of research and review.

Proposing the legislation

The first stage of proposed legislation is generally a 'white paper', a policy document which sets out the main themes in relation to the particular topic or area of concern and the proposed measures needed to improve the situation. This may be a consequence of a working party or Royal Commission report, as outlined above, from responses to a consultative document issued by the Government (a 'green paper') or may stem directly from government sources.

The white paper subsequently forms the basis of a 'bill'. A bill is, in effect, a draft form of legislation. It translates the main points of the white paper into a form of language that is suitable to form the basis of an Act of Parliament. Such language has to be very precise and unambiguous so that scope for misinterpretation is minimized.

Such bills represent official government policy. However, there are also 'Private Members' Bills', proposals for legislation put forward by one or more MPs. These generally relate to a specific area and, because they do not have the weight of the Government behind them, they often fall by the wayside without achieving the status of law. Such bills often stem from pressure groups who manage to find an MP who is sympathetic to their cause and is prepared to support it in this way.

Passing the legislation

For a bill to become law it must be passed by both Houses of Parliament (Commons and Lords) and must also receive the Royal Assent. The bill can be introduced into either house, and will then follow a set procedure:

1. *First reading* This is a formal first reading and acts as a precursor to the printed version being made available.
2. *Second reading* This usually occurs a few weeks after the first reading and is intended as a stimulus for debate and an opportunity for feedback on the proposals.

3. *The Report stage*   This is a period during which amendments can be made.
4. *Third reading*   Following the Report stage, the bill is debated further prior to receiving its third reading.
5. *Transfer to the other House*   Once approved in the House in which it originates, the bill passes to the other House where it goes through a similar set of stages.
6. *Royal Assent*   In principle, the Monarch can object to a bill, but this power of veto has not been exercised since 1707. Once Royal Assent has been given, the bill formally becomes an Act of Parliament and therefore part of the law of the land.

It should be noted that all bills are 'sessional'. That is, if a bill does not complete its passage through to Royal Assent in one session of Parliament, it falls and cannot be continued in the next session of Parliament.

Implementing the legislation

Once an Act is 'on the statute books', plans must then be made to implement it – it does not automatically come into force. This is an important point and one that is often misunderstood. For example, the Children Act 1989 was not implemented until 1991, but this does not prevent some students from writing in their essays: 'Since 1989 the Children Act has required social workers to ... '.

The implementation of an Act of Parliament will often generate a range of related documents and procedural guidelines (to be discussed below).

Interpreting the law

Although the law is often specific and explicit about what can and what cannot be done, there is none the less considerable scope for interpretation. This can be seen to apply at four main levels:

1. *Statutory guidance*   The Government (in the form of the Department of Health, for example) will often issue guidance on how particular pieces of legislation should be applied.
2. *Local policies*   Local authorities or other social work agencies will develop their own policies and procedures in line with their interpretations of the law and its requirements.

3. *Precedent* As we shall see below, the law develops through 'precedent', the interpretation of law in specific court cases setting the baseline from which future decisions will be made.
4. *Direct practice* The law does not dictate precisely how professionals should act in all situations, and so professional discretion is a further stage of interpretation of the law.

The status of legislation

Having considered the process by which legislation comes into being, we can now explore the 'status' of legislation. By this I mean the various aspects of legislation and associated matters which give the law its power and standing.

Powers and duties

First of all it is necessary to be clear about the distinction between powers and duties. A power is something granted to an individual (or the organization employing the individual) which allows him or her to undertake certain steps. For example, various Acts give local authorities the power to provide certain services. That is, they *may* do so but do not necessarily have to. A duty, by contrast, is something that the individual or organization is *obliged* to carry out. For example, under section 47(2) of the Children Act 1989, a local authority is required to enquire into the circumstances of a child where there is reason to believe he or she may be in need of protection from harm. In short, a power says 'may', while a duty says 'must'.

Legal documents

Another important issue to address is the relationship between the law itself and other legal documents. The following brief explanations should be helpful in this regard:

1. *Statute* The actual law or Act of Parliament itself is known as the statute. This is usually a fairly detailed document, which presents the main provisions and any relevant exceptions. Each Act is usually broken down into parts, sections and subsections, allowing us to be quite precise in pinning down exactly where a particular point of law is to be found.

2. *Statutory instruments* These are minor, more specific documents that relate back to their 'parent' Act – that is, the Act of Parliament to which they refer. These are generally refinements of the actual statute, perhaps spelling out in more specific detail one or more provisions of the Act. Such instruments have the status and standing of statute, and therefore have to be treated with the same degree of respect and diligence.

3. *Statutory guidance* This refers to documents issued by the relevant government department (usually the Department of Health in the case of statutes relating to social work). Such volumes of guidance offer advice on good practice in relation to specific aspects of implementation of the Act concerned. Such documents set the expectations for how the provisions of the Act should be dealt with in practice. Such guidance does not have the status of statute, but there is none the less a clear expectation that the guidance will be followed unless there are good reasons why not. It is a very risky business for a social worker or social work agency to ignore the guidance without good reason.

Case law precedent

As mentioned earlier, the law is not a static entity. It develops through the establishment of precedents in case law. This means that, each time a new issue is resolved in court, the outcome sets a precedent. The precedent then becomes the basis for future court decisions relating to such matters.

This process is known officially by its Latin name of *stare decisis,* 'to stand by decisions made'. When a new piece of legislation comes into force, there are, of course, many untested areas that are covered by the general principles of the law but not by specific guidance. As time goes on, the number of untested areas reduces as a body of case law builds up, setting the necessary precedents to guide both future decision-making in the courts and future practice in the professional arena.

The process of developing precedents through case law is therefore an important part of the development of the legal and policy context.

Social policy

As we have seen, the law forms the basis of social work practice. It is a foundation on which so many aspects of practice depend. However, in between the two levels of law and practice lies that of policy. In order to begin to understand this intervening level, I shall explore the important topic of social policy before moving on to consider how agency policies act as a further link in the chain, connecting social policy with actual practice.

What is social policy?

The term 'social policy' is an ambiguous one. It refers to both the range of policies developed in response to social problems and concerns, and the academic discipline dedicated to the study of such policies, their development and effects. My concern here is with the former.

Traditionally, social policy is concerned with five main areas: income maintenance, housing, education, health and personal social services. Each of these areas involves a set of policies geared towards providing a range of services to prevent or respond to social problems and to promote the welfare of citizens. I shall examine each of these areas in turn and comment on their significance for, and links with, social work practice. This will set the scene for a discussion of different approaches to social policy and welfare services.

Income maintenance

This refers to the measures in place to attempt to ensure that everyone has at least a basic level of income sufficient to meet fundamental human needs. This is a key part of the notion of a 'welfare state' – the principle that the state should seek to ensure that there is a finan-cial 'safety net' for the benefit of those who are unable to provide for

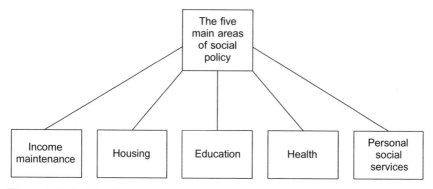

Figure 2.2 Social policy

themselves. It is argued that no-one in a civilized society should be in a position where they cannot afford the basic necessities of life.

In the UK, as in many other countries, income maintenance policies involve a range of insurance-based benefits and a range of others that are not dependent on having made insurance contributions. An example of the former would be unemployment benefit which is paid to people who become unemployed after a period in which they have made a number of national insurance contributions. An example of the latter, by contrast, would be social security payments to someone who is unemployed without having made national insurance contributions – for example, a student who has recently completed a course but has not yet found a job.

Income maintenance, then, is intended to prevent or alleviate poverty, although the debate about what constitutes poverty and how it should be measured is a very complex one (Alcock, 1993). None the less, in whatever way we define it, poverty is a very important issue for social work because:

- a significant proportion of social work clients will be experiencing poverty and deprivation;
- poverty can exacerbate other problems, for example, family relationship difficulties, abuse and mental health problems;
- complications in the welfare benefit system can lead to the need for social workers to provide or arrange welfare rights advice and advocacy;
- self-esteem, confidence and motivation can be adversely affected;
- there are links between poverty and crime; poverty and poor housing; poverty and poor health; and so on;
- sociopolitical class differences can form the basis of discrimination and oppression ('unemployed people are lazy and untrustworthy').

Of course, this is not an exhaustive list, but it should be sufficient to point out the relevance of income maintenance policies for social work.

Housing

The need for shelter is, of course, one of the basic human needs. State policies relating to housing are concerned with a wide range of issues, including the following:

- the provision of local authority ('council') housing at reasonable cost;

- subsidy of housing associations which also provide housing at reasonable cost, particularly for people with special needs (for example, housing that has been adapted to allow wheelchair access);
- subsidy of house purchase through tax relief on mortgages;
- financial support for voluntary agencies which provide accommodation and support for homeless people;
- the provision of warden-supervised sheltered accommodation.

Housing policies have been subject to considerable change over the years, particularly in the 1980s as a result of Margaret Thatcher's strategy of developing a 'home-owning democracy' through the sale of council housing. No doubt there will continue to be changes and developments in housing policy, but it is none the less highly likely that housing will continue to be an important aspect of social policy for social workers.

Housing can be seen to be relevant to social work in a number of ways, including the following:

- Poor quality or overcrowded housing can accentuate social and interpersonal problems – for example, family conflicts or mental health problems.
- Actual or threatened eviction can be a very significant factor in many people's lives.
- Homelessness both presents its own problems and exacerbates existing problems.
- Accommodation has to be adapted for many people in response to specific needs, for example, in relation to disability.
- Neighbour disputes or other forms of harassment often lead to a need for rehousing.

As a result of these factors, social workers frequently find themselves in contact with housing officers in local authorities and housing associations and others involved in housing matters. It pays, therefore, for social workers to be *au fait* with housing policy and related issues.

Education

The state has two sets of responsibilities in relation to education. First, it is a major provider of education in the form of schools, colleges and universities. Second, it plays a key role in regulating education provision, within both its own institutions and those in the private and voluntary sectors.

Education is compulsory for children aged between five and sixteen years of age. For the vast majority of children this involves the need to attend school, although it is possible, in certain circumstances, for dispensation to be given for education to be provided at home.

The provision of education is geared partly towards providing an educated workforce, prepared for the demands of the modern world of work, and partly towards a more general goal of self-improvement and citizenship within a civilized society.

Education policy has a number of implications for social work practice, not least the following:

- Social workers (and/or specialist education welfare officers) are involved in dealing with poor school attendance or school-related problems (for example, bullying).
- Social workers may be involved in a multidisciplinary assessment of a child's educational needs, where the circumstances make this necessary or appropriate.
- Children looked after by the local authority (with foster carers or in residential care) often have difficulties or complications in relation to their schooling.
- Children and adults with learning difficulties may have complex educational needs that require the intervention of a social worker.
- Schools are frequently the sources of child protection referrals, and such work will often involve close liaison with teachers and/or other education staff.

It should be clear, then, that policy relating to education is also likely to be directly or indirectly relevant to social work.

Health

The National Health Service is a major feature of the UK state. It attempts to provide a comprehensive health care service, free at the point of use. Of course, the NHS is not the only provider of health care – there are many private sector providers – nor is the NHS the government's only contribution to health policy. As with education, the state not only provides its own health care services (through the NHS) but also regulates the services provided by others.

Health can be seen as a focal point as far as social policy is concerned. This is because health can have a major bearing on other policy areas (for example, illness obstructing educational progress) and other policy areas can also have a major bearing on health (for example, damp housing exacerbating asthma). Health issues therefore play a central role in social policy.

It is not surprising, then, that health matters impinge on social work practice in a number of ways, including the following:

- Social workers are employed in health care settings, such as hospitals and (less frequently) GP surgeries and health centres.
- Health-related issues are often part of the complex matrix of factors that can lead to the need for social work intervention – in working with older people, for example.
- The stresses arising from social and interpersonal problems can have an adverse effect on health, either through stress-related illnesses (ulcerative colitis, for example) or by aggravating existing medical conditions (angina, for example).
- Health and development issues can be significant factors in the investigation of alleged child abuse (for example, where young children 'fail to thrive').
- Many social problems, such as drug and alcohol addiction, require a multidisciplinary response involving both social workers and health care workers.

The relationship between social work and health care is often complex and sometimes fraught with difficulties. None the less, it should be clear that both areas of practice have much in common and inter-relate in significant ways.

Personal social services

As noted in Chapter 1, social work forms a major part of the personal social services. Policy in this area is therefore directly relevant to the day-to-day concerns of social work staff. For the most part, it can be divided into three broad areas:

- *Child care* This relates to working with children and families, especially children deemed to be 'in need'. This includes children in need of care and protection – or those who may become in need of such care and protection if supportive services are not provided.
- *Community care* The primary aim of community care policy is to prevent the need for institutional care for those people who are unable to cope at home unaided as a result of illness, infirmity,

disability, mental health problems or other such issues. Resources are invested in supporting people within the community in order to avoid or postpone the need for institution-based care.

- *Criminal justice*   Social work services can play an important role in the criminal justice system (including youth justice) by attempting to address the social and personal problems that so often contribute to offending behaviour. Such work is closely associated with the courts system, prisons and young offender institutions.

Of course, this is not an exhaustive list, nor are the categories mutually exclusive. However, this tripartite division should none the less provide a useful overview of the main areas of the personal social services.

These, then, are the five main areas of social policy as generally recognized, although they are not the only ones of relevance to social work. Employment policy and family policy are two further examples that also make a contribution to the policy context of social work. However, space does not permit further consideration of these here. Social workers need to develop their understanding of the policy context far beyond the basics covered here, and so attention is drawn to the 'Guide to further learning' section at the end of the chapter.

Agency policy

In much the same way that social policy involves interpreting and implementing the law, so too does agency policy involve making sense of the broader legal and policy issues and relating them to the realities of practice. Agency policy therefore reflects a further level of 'funnelling' in which broader, more generalized concerns and issues are narrowed down to apply in the specific circumstances of the agency concerned.

How specific a policy can be will depend, to a certain extent at least, on the size of the agency concerned. For example, it will be easier for a small, specialized voluntary organization to have specific, well-defined policies than a large Social Services Department serving a large and diverse geographical area and covering a wide range of services and policy areas.

It is also possible for policies to exist at different levels *within* an agency. For example, a large social services department may have policies that apply throughout the whole of the department, while other policies may vary from district to district within the authority.

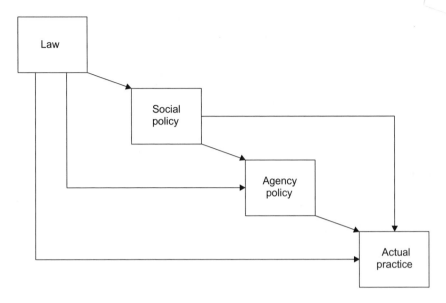

Figure 2.3 'Filtered' influences on practice

This represents a further step in the process of narrowing and filtering referred to above and also illustrated in Figure 2.3.

In considering agency policy, it is also important to consider the extent to which policies are *operationalized* – that is, translated into action. Unfortunately, it is not uncommon for policies to exist on paper only, in the sense that they form part of the official policy of the agency concerned but are not actually acted upon. For example, an organization may have an equal opportunity policy geared towards eradicating discrimination, and yet may actually operate in ways that are far from egalitarian. In extreme cases, staff may not even know that certain policies exist, such is the limited context of operationalization.

One means by which policies can be operationalized is through a set of procedures. A clear example of this approach is the use of child protection procedures to guide practice in responding to suspected or actual child abuse. Such procedures take the form of a document agreed at a local level on a multidisciplinary basis by the various agencies involved in child protection work (social services, health, education and police).

This document will provide guidance on:

- how suspicious allegations or instances of abuse should be reported;
- how such matters should be investigated;

- when and how a medical examination should take place;
- when a case conference should be organized and how;

and so on.

In some respects, these procedures take the form of general guidelines that leave a lot of room for professional discretion. In other respects, they can be quite prescriptive at times, spelling out what *must* happen in certain circumstances. It is very important to be able to distinguish between the two, as a failure to follow a specific, explicit instruction can result in a disciplinary charge, even if no harm comes to a child as a result of not adhering to the procedures.

Although agency procedures, and policy guidelines more broadly, are very important factors in shaping the translation of policy into practice, they are not the only ones. Another important factor is that of organizational culture. This refers to the sets of common patterns, assumptions, values and norms that become established within an organization over a period of time. It is summed up in the phrase: 'the way we do things around here'.

An organization's culture can be very subtle and largely imperceptible, especially for staff who have worked there for a long time and have grown so accustomed to it that it seems natural and inevitable. Indeed, it is often when someone moves from one organization to another that the significance of organizational culture becomes apparent – when he or she realizes just how different the new organization is from the old one, not necessarily in any major ways, but in lots and lots of little ways.

We can see from this, then, that an organization's culture can be a major influence on the operationalization of policy, largely because it tends to be such a strong influence on organizational behaviour in general. For example, where there is a culture of defensiveness (where people are unlikely to take risks – see Chapter 6), it follows that policies will be implemented defensively. Similarly, in an organization with a culture characterized by a strong commitment to learning, policies relating to training and staff development are likely to be more fully operationalized than would otherwise be the case in other settings.

Organizational culture arises from 'custom and practice'. That is, habits and patterns that establish themselves over a period of time become so ingrained that they form part of the fabric of the organization. This can have a number of implications, including the following:

- Some established patterns may not be entirely compatible with areas of law and policy. For example, community care policy encourages creative responses to areas of identified need but many organizations have a culture that is not conducive to innovative thinking.
- Some aspects of practice may be emphasized at the expense of others as a result of the norms prevalent within a particular organization. For example, a social work agency may place a great deal of emphasis on emergency work and relatively little on preventative work.
- A number of 'taboo' or 'no-go' areas may be established. For example, some cultures discourage discussion of emotional issues, even though these may be central to the work being undertaken.
- There may be a clash between one organization's culture and another's. For example, in multidisciplinary work, conflicts and tensions may arise because of the different 'styles' of the organizations concerned.
- An organization's culture is often gender-biased. For example, some organizations have a distinctly 'macho' approach to their work.

Clearly, then, the patterns that develop as part of an organization's culture can be very significant and influential in terms of how broader levels of law and policy take shape in the day-to-day realities of practice.

Professional practice

As I commented in Chapter 1, professional practice necessarily involves a degree of discretion and judgement. That is, social work is much more than following rules or procedures – at each step judgements have to be formed and decisions made. Consequently, we have to recognize that, despite the various 'layers' of the legal and policy context, there is still a considerable degree of autonomy (although working in a large bureaucracy can often give the misleading – and potentially dangerous – impression that there is little or no autonomy). It is therefore not enough to consider the legal and policy context in the abstract – we also need to consider the relationship between that context and actual practice.

Interpretation

Although the influence of law and policy is very strong indeed, laws and policies have to be *interpreted* – they do not spell out in fine detail what needs to be done. For example, the NHS and Community Care Act 1990 speaks of 'people who are in need of community care services', but this is a very imprecise term that requires a great deal of interpretation. What exactly does 'in need of community care services' mean? How do we determine who is, and who is not, in need of such services? These are matters that have to be addressed directly in concrete situations, rather than dealt with at a generalized abstract level. Such matters are resolved at a very practical day-to-day level as social workers go about their business.

Similarly, the Children Act 1989 uses the concept of 'children in need' but the question of who comes into that category is left largely to interpretation on a case-by-case basis. It is simply not possible (or desirable) to legislate in such fine detail as to remove altogether the need for interpretation. As Braye and Preston-Shoot (1997) emphasize, using the law in practice is neither simple nor unproblematic.

Use of knowledge

Law and policy issues are complex and wide ranging. Although practitioners clearly need at least a basic understanding of the relevant knowledge base, it would be unrealistic to expect a thorough and comprehensive knowledge of all aspects of the law and policy. It is for this reason that:

- Law and policy issues must feature strongly in professional education and training.
- We must recognize that changes in the law produce new training needs, as staff need to keep abreast of developments in the knowledge base.
- We must accept that mistakes will be made from time to time as a result of gaps in practitioners' knowledge.
- Practitioners must know how to find out about legal knowledge in terms of reference books, policy and guidance, consultation with managers and legal advisors and so on.

The extent to which legal and policy requirements will be met in practice will therefore depend, to a certain extent at least, on how effectively and appropriately practitioners use their knowledge of the law. The law is certainly far from perfect, but what makes it even more imperfect is the fact that its effective implementation relies on practitioners' use of an enormous knowledge base.

Use of skills

A similar argument can be drawn upon in relation to the use of skills. Implementing law and policy is a skilled activity. For example, in using the law, the skills involved in gathering and presenting evidence can be crucial. An application for a Care Order in respect of an abused child can depend a great deal on the credibility of the social worker concerned, especially if the application is contested by parents.

Skills, of course, owe much to experience, confidence, supervision and training, and so the use of skills forms another significant variable in how legal and policy mandates are translated into actual practice. This reinforces an important theme: that the relationship between the legal and policy context and day-to-day practice is not a direct, simple or straightforward one.

Use of values

Of course, law and policy are not neutral or value free. They reflect particular sets of values. For example, the value of the family is clearly a major feature of child care legislation. However, this is not to say that the practitioner's own values do not also feature in the use of law and policy in practice.

Chapter 5 is devoted to the question of the role of values in social work, and I shall be arguing there that our own values inevitably influence how we carry out our tasks. It is therefore an oversimplification to see the legal and policy context as a set of rules and procedures to follow. Social work is not that mechanistic, and practitioners constantly find themselves in situations where they have to make decisions based on values. For example, in working with children, the extent to which we value children's right to be consulted will have a major bearing on how we work in such cases (Thomas, 2000). Values, therefore, play an important role in the relationship between the legal and policy context and practice in terms of the following:

- Values are implicit (if not explicit) within law and policy, and these tend to reflect the dominant values within society.
- Our own values can influence the way we interpret and implement law and policy.

- At times there may be a clash between the values underpinning the law or policy and those of the practitioner.

Accountability

Because law and policy do not provide detailed prescriptions for practice, individual social workers have to take responsibility for their actions. That is, they are accountable. Although law and policy are very influential in shaping practice, it is still the decisions and actions of individual practitioners that form the basis of actual practice – and it is these that render the social worker accountable.

In short, professional practice is accountable practice, precisely because law and policy do not prescribe exactly what should happen – this is down to the judgement and professionalism of the practitioner.

The limits of the law

This follows on from the previous point, namely the importance of recognizing that the law does not provide precise prescriptions for practice. However, we can take this a step further in recognizing that there are many aspects of practice where law and policy have only a limited influence. For example, Dalrymple and Burke (1995) make the point that, in responding to elder abuse, social workers have little or no recourse to the law and are, in effect, sailing through relatively uncharted waters.

We therefore have to see law and policy in perspective. In many ways they are very influential indeed, but for some areas of practice they have only a limited bearing on what is largely left to professional discretion.

Conclusion

This chapter has shown that the law arises as a result of complex political processes, and, once in place and implemented, it is a major factor in:

- shaping social policy at a national and local level, and agency policy within individual organizations;
- influencing priorities within social work agencies;
- determining the relationship between the state and the private and voluntary sectors;

- determining the relationship between different 'arms' of the state, for example between health and personal social services;
- reinforcing the dominant values and ideas within a society;
- setting the context for professional practice;
- acting as a basis, in many cases, of deciding the appropriateness or otherwise of particular courses of action;
- preventing certain steps from being taken;
- making agencies and individual practitioners accountable for their practice;
- acting as a motor force of change in social policy more broadly and professional practice more specifically.

Clearly it has been possible to cover only the basic features of the legal and policy context of social work. The Guide to further learning section below should be consulted for guidance as to how to develop the more in-depth knowledge that social workers need to have.

This context is a very complex one, and one that constantly changes as a result of new laws, developments in policies and political changes. It is therefore important that social workers keep up to date with developments in the legal and policy issues that affect practice. To study such matters as part of one's qualifying training and then to pay little or no attention to developments in subsequent years is clearly a recipe for disaster.

Guide to further learning

There are a number of books that provide an overview of the law relating to social work. For example, Brayne *et al.* (2001), Ball and McDonald (2002) and Braye and Preston-Shoot (1997) do a good job of addressing the complexities and intricacies of putting the law into practice, particularly in the context of anti-oppressive practice, while Preston-Shoot (1998) provides a good summary and overview of the law relating to discrimination. Cooper and Vernon (1996) provide an overview of the law relating to disability issues, while Griffiths and Roberts (1995) cover the law relating to older people, and Hoggett (1996) covers mental health law. White *et al.* (1990) includes the full text of the Children Act 1989 and a useful commentary on it. Baillie *et al.* (2003) is a useful text on social work law in Scotland. The Human Rights Act is covered in Wadham and Mountfield (1999) and Watson and Wolfe (2003).

In relation to social policy, Alcock (1996), Blakemore (1998) and Baldock *et al.* (2003) provide helpful introductory texts. Williams (1989), although now rather dated, provides a more critical, anti-discriminatory perspective whilch is well worth consulting. Ungerson and Kember (1997) provide a helpful set of readings which cast light on some of the gender implications of social policy. Ahmad and Atkin (1996) address community care issues with a focus on racial aspects. Thompson and Thompson (2005) offer an account of community care policy.

Exercise 2

For this exercise, you will need to identify three pieces of legislation that are relevant to social work practice, and, for each one, consider:

1. What are the main *duties* this Act places upon social workers?
2. What are the main *powers* this Act bestows upon social workers?

For this exercise you may need to consult some of the literature mentioned above in the 'Guide to further learning' section, or you may need to seek advice from an experienced social worker. Use the space below to make some notes.

3

The knowledge base

Introduction

In Chapter 2 it was emphasized that, although the legal and policy context is an extremely important influence on practice, it does not prescribe in fine detail how we should proceed in any particular situation – there is still considerable professional autonomy, in the sense that the individual social worker has to make decisions about what he or she does. Social work cannot be done in a mechanical, unthinking way (even though, as I shall be arguing in Chapter 6, many people do in fact attempt this, with very harmful results). It is therefore necessary to have a knowledge base to draw upon so that we are not reinventing the wheel every time we act. The knowledge base represents, to a large extent, the consolidated knowledge of practitioners, theorists and researchers who have covered similar ground in the past and have left us the legacy of their experiences and learning. This does not mean that we have to take their experiences and learning at face value and accept them wholesale, but it does mean that we would be very foolish to ignore this knowledge base and start from scratch each day, failing to learn from other people's mistakes and successes.

This knowledge base is a very large and complex one, and one that is developing all the time as a result of developments in practice, theory, policy and research, and of course changes in the social, economic and political circumstances in which social problems occur. It would clearly be unrealistic, then, to attempt to present the whole of the social work knowledge base in one chapter (or even one book!). My aim here is therefore a more modest one. What I present here is, first an overview of what the knowledge base consists of (but even this is not comprehensive) and, second, a discussion of what sort of approach needs to be taken to the knowledge base, and finally a discussion of what problems can arise if the knowledge base available to social workers is not drawn upon, or is not used appropriately or effectively. I shall begin, then, by mapping out the terrain of the social work knowledge base.

What do social workers need to know?

This is a big question! In order to try and answer it I shall break down the knowledge base into a number of sub-sections and consider each of these in turn. It is important to emphasize, though, that there is nothing definitive about the way I have categorized elements of knowledge here. Other writers may use different categories, but it is not a question of which systems of categories are right or wrong. Rather, it is a matter of using a category system to break down a very complex whole into manageable chunks for ease of understanding. These 'chunks' are not necessarily separate in reality – indeed they generally overlap and intertwine in subtle and intricate ways and often influence each other. The categories, then, are intended as aids to understanding, rather than as a definitive way of dividing up the elements of knowledge. As Chapter 2 was devoted specifically to issues relating to the legal and policy context, I shall not repeat here a discussion of the part they play in the underpinning knowledge base of social work. The categories of knowledge presented here should therefore be seen as in addition to those of the legal and policy context.

Human development

How to intervene in a particular situation will depend, of course, on a number of factors, but one set of issues that is often to the fore is that of human development – matters relating to the human life course. For example, the response to a child will be different from that to a middle-aged adult, or to an older adult. Similarly, we would respond differently in dealing with a five-year old than we would in dealing with a fifteen-year old. This is because we recognize the significance of the life course as an influence in people's lives and acknowledge that people will face different challenges and issues, depending on where they are on that life course.

The life course has a number of implications for us as we grow and develop, as the stage of the life course we have reached will tend to be an important contextual factor in making sense of the problems and challenges we face and the range of potential solutions. The stages of the life course are presented differently by different theorists, but for present purposes, I shall outline them as follows:

- *Infancy* The very early stages of life during which we are very dependent upon others for protection and nurturance. This is also a very significant stage in terms of our psychological development in so far as experiences at this stage can have a profound effect on our view of the world and how we respond to it in later years.
- *Childhood* As we grow from infancy we begin the process of becoming more independent, although we still need a good deal of protection and nurturance. Again, this developmental stage can be highly significant in shaping our psychological responses and attitudes.
- *Adolescence* As we move from childhood to adulthood, we go through a transitional period known as 'adolescence'. This is often portrayed as a time of 'storm and stress', although, in reality, the majority of young people pass through adolescence without too much difficulty or drama (Lipsitz, 1980). This is, none the less, an important time in life, as it is often at this time that people develop career plans or other ideas about the direction they want their lives to go in.
- *Early adulthood* This is generally seen as a stage when people are establishing themselves in the adult world, through work, sexual relationships, setting up home, having children and so on.
- *Middle age* This is seen as a time of life when patterns are more established and are characterized by maturity and experience. It is generally seen as a period of consolidation.
- *Old age* As I shall argue below, old age is often stereotyped in negative terms as a period of dependency, frailty and inability to cope. The reality is very different for most older people.
- *Death* Death is not always recognized as a stage in the life course. Indeed, death-related issues are often neglected, as if they were a taboo subject. Death is none the less a very significant part of the life course.

An understanding of the life course is a necessary prerequisite for social workers in a number of ways, not least the following:

1. In order to form an understanding of the person or persons being helped, it is important to appreciate what stage of the life course they have reached and what this means to them.

2. The problems social workers encounter are often stage related, for example, child abuse cases often relate to the neglect of a dependent infant who relies on parental nurturance to survive.
3. Problems may arise where people have difficulty making the adjustment from one life stage to the next, adolescence being a common example. Crisis intervention, to be discussed below, is closely related to this phenomenon.
4. Different people may experience the life course in different ways as a result of disability or other social factors.

This final point is particularly important, as there is a danger of the life course being used as a rigid framework that people are expected to fit into (and are defined as 'deviant' if they do not). The life course describes what is 'normal' in the sense of what is usual, statistically. It does not mean that other groups or individuals who do not fit this pattern are necessarily 'abnormal' in the sense of having or being a problem. Indeed, we have to recognize that the traditional approach to the life course is potentially very oppressive, as it has a tendency to discriminate against people who do not fit the general pattern (people with disabilities, gay men and lesbians and so on), and also often fails to take account of important gender and cultural differences. It should therefore be remembered that the life course is a means of beginning to understand common stages of development and is not a rigid framework for making judgements about 'abnormality'. This is an important point about the use of knowledge generally and one to which I shall return below.

Another important point to recognize is that the life course is not simply a matter of biology. Clearly, there is a biological dimension to it, for example in relation to the dependency associated with infancy. However, we should be wary of overestimating the role of biology in the life course. There are also psychological, social, political and existential dimensions that have to be considered (Thompson, 1995a). Indeed, the existential dimension can be seen as very important, for each stage of the life course brings with it new existential challenges – new problems to solve as we cope with the day-to-day realities of our existence.

A very important and unifying theme in relation to the life course is that of identity, the sense of self we develop and maintain throughout our lives. Identity is not a fixed entity, nor is it a matter entirely beyond our control. Identity represents an ongoing interaction between the individual and his or her personal and social circumstances – it is our 'biography' that we write, metaphorically speaking, as we move through life, making sense of the situations we encounter, integrating the influences on us and maintaining a sense of coherence and continuity. Problems associated with identity (for example, low self-esteem) are commonly encountered in social work practice.

Social processes and institutions

It is no coincidence that the term 'social worker' begins with the word *social*. The social context is a vitally important part of the situations social workers encounter and are expected to respond to. This applies in a number of ways, including the following:

- Many of the problems encountered are social in origin, for example as a result of poverty and deprivation or racial harassment.
- Social problems are *socially constructed*. That is, they are defined by society. For example, some issues are defined as illegal in some countries but not in others (prostitution, for example).
- Potential solutions are often at a social or community level, rather than individual (poverty again being a good example) and may involve the social worker in putting pressure on others to deal with the problem (through community action, for example), rather than dealing with it directly.
- Responding to social work problems often involves drawing on wider social resources (local government services, for example).
- Personal or psychological factors do not exist in a vacuum – they are strongly influenced and constrained by social issues.
- There can be social consequences as a result of being involved with a social worker (stigma, for example).
- Social work intervention can have the effect of exacerbating social inequalities, for example by reinforcing gender stereotypes.
- The social policies that govern social work interventions have their roots in the social, political and economic circumstances of the day.

It is therefore important for social workers to have an understanding of the social context of their work. To ignore the social dimension is to ignore a major feature of the social work world and of the reality of the circumstances of clients.

This does not mean that social workers need to be experts in sociology but they do need at least a basic grounding in understanding how society works in terms of social processes and institutions. This involves recognizing the significance of:

- *Social divisions* Class, race, ethnicity, gender, age, disability, sexual identity, religion and so on are important ways in which people's lives are influenced and constrained by social factors relating to the distribution of opportunities and life chances. It is no coincidence that the majority of social work clients are to be found in low-income groups. Similarly, it is not surprising that the majority of clients are women, given that women are expected to take a lead role on managing the family and household (see the discussion below of ideology).

- *Power* Power is a very complex issue and operates at a number of different levels. However, from a social work point of view, it is extremely important in so far as social work clients are generally in relatively low positions of power, as a result of either their social location (in relation to the 'social divisions' outlined above) or the particular problem they face that brings them into contact with a social worker (a drink problem, for example), or indeed a combination of both. In addition, social work interventions themselves involve the exercise of power, and this can be used positively to *empower* clients or negatively to reinforce the disadvantages they suffer.

- *Ideology* Ideology refers to the power of ideas to maintain existing structures and social relations. For example, patriarchal ideology (patriarchy means 'the law of the father' – that is, male dominance) serves to maintain existing power relations between men and women by presenting gender roles as natural and inevitable (despite the considerable evidence to the contrary). Ideology is closely linked to power because it is largely through the role of ideology that power is exercised. That is, the subtle, often unquestioned, workings of ideology can be far more effective in maintaining power structures than the overt and explicit use of power, for example through force or coercion.

- *Law and order* As we saw in Chapter 2, the law is part of the social fabric, a major feature of how social stability is maintained. Law and order are important features of social life, as it is through the exercise of law, both within and outside the court system, that much of social life is regulated. This places social workers in a significant, if often uncomfortable position, as social work is part of the law and order machinery geared towards maintaining social stability, but also involves working towards social amelioration by working with some of the most vulnerable and disadvantaged groups in society.

- *Social institutions*   This is a term that refers to those enduring and relatively stable features of society, the metaphorical building blocks of the social order. These include marriage, the family, the work ethic, religion, education and national identity. These are closely linked to ideology and play a major role in giving us a sense of the 'shape' of our society, the factors that are significant in helping us recognize how society works all around us. These are not 'natural' features of society and often vary from society to society.

The social context of social work is indeed vast and it can be quite challenging for social workers to keep abreast of all that they need to know, especially as social change can occur quite rapidly. However, the following questions should prove useful in helping practitioners be aware of the relevance of social processes and institutions:

1. *What is the social location of the person(s) you are dealing with?* That is, how do factors like class, race, gender, age or disability affect the situation? What is the cultural context? Is there a (potential) clash between their social location and yours? For example, do you speak the same language or will you need an interpreter?
2. *What social factors may have contributed to the problem situation?* What is the role of poverty, poor housing, social stigma, discrimination and so on?
3. *In dealing with a family, are there any social differences that could be significant* within *the family?*   Are there issues to do with gender roles or expectations? Is an older or disabled member of the family being marginalized or exploited in some way?
4. *In responding to a problem in a particular way, could you be exacerbating existing social inequalities or disadvantages?*   Could you be reinforcing racism by being insensitive to cultural needs and differences? Could you be guilty of exacerbating ageism by failing to deal with an older person with respect and dignity?
5. *If the roots of the problem are in the broader social or political sphere, is there anything you can do to influence that wider sphere?*   For example, could you bring the matter to the attention of the relevant authorities or pressure groups who are concerned with such issues?

These will not give you all you need to know, but they will at least give you a starting point, an entry into the complexities of the social context.

Interpersonal, group and organizational dynamics

Many of the problems social workers are concerned with have much to do with the interactions of people, whether at an interpersonal, group or organizational level. It is important, then, for practitioners to have an understanding of what is involved in such interactions. Once again we find ourselves in very complex territory, with an enormous literature and research base, not to mention considerable practice wisdom built up over many decades of professional practice. The comments here, then, are necessarily selective.

At an interpersonal level, we can see that interactions between people are, in many ways, the nuts and bolts of social work, and indeed of the human services more broadly. What, then, are the important factors of which we need to be aware in seeking to understand interpersonal interactions? The following are some of the main sets of issues that apply:

- *Communication* Styles and patterns of communication can be very significant indeed. Of course, we need to consider not only verbal communication (what is said) but also non-verbal communication (the 'body language' that accompanies speech). The words we use, the tone of voice, the speed at which we speak, the gestures we use, the pauses and silences and the things we *do not* say can all be very significant indeed in determining how other people see us and how they respond to us. Similarly, it is also important that we become skilled in 'reading' other people's communications, effective listeners who are able to put people at ease and work effectively with them.

- *Power* Once again power features as an aspect of this part of social work. Power relations are generally reflected in interpersonal interactions and can be reinforced or challenged by such interactions. For example, a person in a position of power may 'talk down' to someone who is relatively less powerful. Who speaks first, who decides the agenda, who speaks most, who concludes the interaction can all be matters decided by reference to power. Power is not just an abstract concept but also exists at a very practical, concrete level in our day-to-day interactions. It is important, then, that social workers are aware of, and sensitive to, the power issues involved in interpersonal interactions so that they contribute to empowerment, rather than reinforce a sense of powerlessness.

- *Context* The context in which interactions take place is also very important, as the setting can have a significant bearing on the process and outcome of the interaction. For example, a conversation that takes place in a formal setting (a case conference, for example) is likely to be heavily influenced by the context. We cannot expect clients to feel comfortable in a formal meeting unless we have taken the necessary steps to prepare them for what is to come, to understand the process and their role and so on.

The same three headings can also be applied to group interactions:

- *Communication* Channels of communication in groups can be very significant. Some members may speak openly and freely, while others may have little or nothing to say. This may be because some feel the way the group works makes it easy for them to contribute, while others may feel inhibited by aspects of the group's functioning or the atmosphere created. It is therefore necessary to have a good understanding of group dynamics, to appreciate the patterns that frequently emerge in groups.
- *Power* The workings of power are often visible in groups, with perhaps one or more individuals trying to dominate, while others are marginalized or excluded altogether, thus reflecting their respective power positions within the group.
- *Context* Settings are also important for group interactions. For example, if there are distractions in the room, this may affect the effectiveness of the group in achieving their aims.

Group interactions also have the added dimension of the fact that a group can appear to take on a life of its own – the whole becomes greater than the sum of its parts. Understanding group interactions is therefore more than simply 'adding up' the interpersonal interactions of those present. There is also the important consideration of interactions *between* groups and factions. Indeed, it is as well to remember that the question of group interactions applies not only to groupwork (in the sense of organized processes of group-based therapy) but also to a whole range of group activities, including family dynamics, teamwork, meetings or training courses.

Organizational dynamics clearly owe much to interpersonal and group dynamics within the organization. However, there can also be other factors operating in the organizational context that have a bearing on interactions. These factors include:

- *the organizational culture* – the 'way we do things around here', patterns established over a long period of time;
- *formal and informal power relations* – the 'official' hierarchy, as well as the less official patterns of power and influence that develop in organizations;
- *policies and procedures* – formal expectations as to how people should act (and interact);
- *management styles* – leadership styles (ranging from authoritarian to democratic) can influence interactions quite significantly.

Because social work practice takes place in an organizational context (in terms of both the employing organization and other relevant organizations or agencies), the complexities of organizational life are likely to impinge a great deal on day-to-day practice, making this another important aspect of the social work knowledge base.

One of the difficulties of understanding interactions is that we are usually part of the dynamic that we are trying to understand. That is, it can be difficult to adopt an objective picture when we are part of the situation we are trying to understand. It is therefore important that, at times, we work together on such matters so that we have the opportunity to 'check out' our own part in the situations we are dealing with. Supervision with our line manager can also be very valuable in this respect.

The social work process

One of the common, if not always justified, criticisms of social work is that of vagueness and drift. According to this view, social work is characterized by a lack of precision about what is to be achieved or how it can or should be achieved. Objectives are seen as vague or non-existent and progress towards them tends to be at best slow and, at worst, confused and misguided. While this view is perhaps something of a caricature, there is no doubt that it does have some basis in truth. For example, investigations into poor practice and court actions against social workers and/or agencies often reveal a lack of clarity and focus at the heart of the problem.

In order for social workers to avoid this vagueness and drift, what is required is what I have referred to elsewhere as 'systematic practice' (Thompson, 2002a). This involves being clear about the objectives of the particular piece of work (what is to be achieved), the strategy for achieving them (how it is to be achieved) and how termination of the work will be determined (What will success look like? How will we know whether or not we are succeeding?). Such systematic practice can be achieved within a five-stage process, as follows:

1. *Assessment* This involves gathering information and forming a picture of what the problems are, what strengths can be drawn upon, what needs to be done, and so on. It is the beginning stage because it is on the basis of this assessment that future work will be undertaken. It is important to note that assessment is not simply about gathering information, nor is it simply about identifying needs or what services should be provided. Assessment is an holistic process that involves gaining an overview of the situation – what is sometimes referred to as 'helicopter vision'. A narrow or superficial assessment can lead to considerable difficulty later when practice may be totally out of keeping with what is needed as a result of the neglect of assessment.

2. *Intervention* Once problems and other relevant factors have been identified, the next step is to make the necessary arrangements to solve those problems, meet the needs and so on. As we shall see below, there are a number of ways in which such intervention can be handled, but the overall process is one of trying to respond to the identified problems in a positive and constructive way. There is no definitive 'right answer' as to how to proceed (see Reflective practice below), although some ways are clearly more appropriate and helpful than others. As I shall emphasize in Chapter 5, it is important that practice should be based on *partnership*. That is, it should seek to involve clients and carers as fully as possible, so that social work becomes a process of doing things *with* people, rather than *to* them. Approaches to intervention should therefore seek to build a partnership, rather than seek a 'cure' for the situation as if the social worker were a 'social doctor'.

3. *Review* Situations change over time, and so our assessments need to change too. Also, it is not uncommon for initial assessments to be incorrect or inaccurate in some way, especially as they some-times have to be based, for a variety of reasons, on fairly limited information. It is therefore important that practice is reviewed periodically so that the necessary adjustments can be made to the social work plan. In some cases, it may be necessary to abandon the plan altogether. However, if work is not reviewed, then it is possible for a great deal of time, effort and energy to be wasted because efforts are being misdirected.

4. *Ending*   In some respects, the aim of social work is to make the social worker redundant. That is, the aim is to enable people to solve their own problems and address their own issues without the need for social work support. In general, then, we should, at all times, be geared towards bringing our intervention to a close. An open-ended approach with little or no appreciation of timescales, progress and priorities can be a major factor in allowing vagueness and drift to creep in. It is therefore important to take seriously the skills involved in bringing intervention to a close, as it is an aspect of practice that can easily be mishandled, thus undoing a lot of good work that has gone before.

5. *Evaluation*   Once the work is completed, we then have the opportunity to learn from it by considering what went well (How can we build on our strengths?), what could have gone better (How can we learn from our mistakes?) and generally what lessons there are to be learned from the experience. Thus evaluation is a fundamental part of good practice, as it provides us with a platform from which to continue to improve. No matter how skilled, experienced or effective we are, there are, of course, always lessons to be learned, improvements to be made and benefits to be gained from evaluating our practice.

It should be noted that the aim of the social work process and systematic practice is not to turn social workers into robots who slavishly follow a rigid sequence of stages, but rather into thinking practitioners who have a framework on which to base their work and the confidence, insight and sensitivity to adapt that framework as and when this becomes necessary. That is, systematic practice is presented as a basis for flexible and reflective professional practice, rather than as an alternative to it.

Theoretical paradigms

As we have seen, the knowledge base of social work is vast and constantly growing. Many people have attempted to make sense of this through developing theoretical approaches, and such work continues to be a feature of the social work academic world. It would, of course, be unrealistic to expect one theoretical approach to provide all the answers we need. We therefore need a grasp of a range of theoretical perspectives and the ability to draw on these as and when required.

Developing a comprehensive typology of social work theories is certainly a task that is far beyond the scope of this book, although I am, more realistically, able to provide an overview of the theoretical trends that have influenced social work over the years and continue to vie for dominance in explaining some of the complexities of identifying the social work task and the consequent attempts to achieve it as effectively and appropriately as possible. What follows, then, is a very brief and simple account of some of the major theoretical schools of social work, my aim being to provide an overview of the range of theoretical frameworks and concepts that are commonly brought to bear in trying to make sense of social work. The main approaches to social work theory and practice are primarily the following:

- *Psychodynamics* Psychodynamic theory derives largely but not exclusively from the work of Sigmund Freud. It relates to the internal psychological conflicts between the irrational pleasure drives of the *id* and the social conscience of the *superego,* mediated by the *ego* or psychological 'regulator'. That is, this approach to social work sees social work problems as owing much to a conflict between the wishes and needs of the individual and the constraints and requirements of society. Practice is therefore mainly a matter of strengthening the *ego* in order to control the demands of the *id* which may be leading the individual concerned into trouble and conflict. Although no longer a dominant approach, it still has some adherents and a degree of influence.
- *Psychosocial casework* This is, in many ways, a development from psychodynamic theory, particularly the ego psychology of writers such as Erikson. The difference between this and psychodynamics proper is that there is here a greater emphasis on the social dimension, the range of social factors that play a part in the social work situation. This means that practice should be geared not only towards psychological adjustments but also towards attempts to alter the social environment or circumstances of the individual or family concerned. As with psychodynamics, this is no longer a dominant approach, although it is still quite influential in some quarters.
- *Humanistic psychology* The focus of humanistic psychology is human potential and the social and psychological barriers that stand in its way. Humans are seen as basically good, and will only tend toward evil when other circumstances thwart and frustrate their potential. The social work task, then, as far as humanistic

psychology is concerned, is to liberate people from these barriers so that their natural goodness can flow through. This has never achieved the status of a dominant approach but its influence none the less continues to be felt in some areas of theory and practice.

- *Behavioural social work* The basic idea behind behavioural social work is that, as behaviour is deemed to be learned through a small number of psychological processes (reinforcement, for example), behaviour-related problems can be solved through interventions that alter the learning process so that problematic behaviours are eradicated (or reduced) while positive behaviours are encouraged. This has been a popular approach in some aspects of practice, although it is no longer as popular as it once was.

- *Systems theory* This is a more explicitly sociological approach in which social work situations are understood as a series of inter-locking social systems (the family system, the neighbourhood system and so on). The task of the social worker, then, is to understand the interactions of such systems and the problems that arise, so that the pattern of systems can be altered and the problems resolved. Family therapy owes much to this approach. The emphasis is on changing the family system as a whole, rather than working with individual factors.

- *Radical social work* This approach grew out of a dissatisfaction with approaches that took little or no account of wider social factors, particularly class, poverty and deprivation. The focus of radical social work was politicization, helping clients develop an awareness of how their problems were linked to social and political factors so that, ultimately, they could contribute to a process of radical social change. There are elements of radical social work still to be found in some modern approaches geared towards empowerment and emancipation (see 'emancipatory practice' below) but radical social work proper arose in the late 1960s but did not survive in any substantial form much beyond the 1980s.

- *Emancipatory practice* Building on the sociopolitical emphasis of radical social work, modern emancipatory approaches to social work are concerned with oppression, recognizing that the majority of social work clients are likely to be exposed to one or more forms of discrimination. The focus of such work is to contribute to the empowerment of clients to help them overcome the disadvantages they experience as a result of their social location and negative attitudes towards them. This is the approach on which the remainder of this book will be premised.

Of course, it is not expected that social workers will have a grasp of all these theoretical perspectives. Some practitioners are well versed in one or more of these theories but have little knowledge of, or interest in, the others. This is not necessarily a problem. The aim is one of developing well-informed practice, rather than persuading practitioners to adopt one theoretical perspective or other. The discussion below of Using knowledge should help to clarify this.

Methods of intervention

The methods of intervention that can be brought to bear in achieving social work aims can be closely linked to the theoretical perspectives outlined above. However, there are also other ways of looking at methods of intervention, for example in terms of whether they are targeted at individuals, families, groups or communities:

- *Individual casework* This is a common form of practice and involves working on a one-to-one basis with clients in order to help resolve their difficulties.
- *Family work* Work can also be geared to working with whole families, trying to create change at the familial, rather than individual, level.
- *Groupwork* This can be a very effective way of working with people who have common problems or concerns. The social worker acts as a facilitator in encouraging the group to support each other in resolving their difficulties.
- *Community work* A far less popular approach than was previously the case, but still alive and well in some areas. The social worker seeks to act as a catalyst in helping community groups to address problems and marshal their resources.

These different 'levels' of intervention are, of course, not mutually exclusive, as they can overlap to a considerable extent. For example, groupwork may be used as part of community work, or individual casework may be undertaken in tandem with family work.

There are a number of methods of intervention commonly used, as the following list should illustrate:

- *Task-centred practice* This involves working together to: (1) clarify the current situation (where you are now – point A) and to identify the preferred alternative situation (where you would like to be – point B); (2) plot the route from A to B in terms of the steps that would have to be taken (the tasks that would have to be achieved), beginning with the easiest in order to boost confidence and establish a basis of success; and (3) agree a shared allocation of the tasks.

- *Contract work* This is very similar to task-centred practice, but uses a negotiated written agreement as the focus of intervention.
- *Crisis intervention* Turning points in people's lives generate a lot of energy that can be used positively to tackle problems, resolve difficulties and move beyond previous barriers to progress. The task of the social worker is to help channel the energies positively before they start to dissipate as the crisis subsides.
- *Counselling* Although in-depth counselling tends to occur only in specialist agencies, social work practice often involves an element of counselling in terms of helping people understand their situation, their feelings and their options.
- *Care management* This involves overseeing the provision of a 'package' of care services geared towards maintaining someone in the community who would otherwise need to rely on institutional provision.
- *Advocacy* Being an advocate involves representing the interests of people who are unable to do so for themselves (for example, as a result of learning difficulties or mental health problems).
- *Mediation* This refers to the work done in helping 'warring factions' (family members, for example) to reconcile their differences by retaining a neutral stance between them.

This is not an exhaustive list, and there are many forms of good practice that do not fit neatly into a theoretical category. Similarly, it is possible for some of these methods and theoretical perspectives to be combined (for example, using behavioural methods in the context of task-centred practice, or using psychodynamic approaches as the basis of counselling). Methods can also be used across levels of intervention. For example, although crisis intervention is generally used with individuals and families in crisis, it can also be used with groups or communities at certain times.

Some practitioners claim not to use specific techniques or methods, but rather prefer to use a mixture which they refer to as 'eclectic'. Sometimes, this amounts to very high-quality practice where the social worker concerned succeeds in integrating elements of theoretical knowledge appropriately and effectively. However, it can also amount to a 'fudge' in which the term 'eclectic' is used in an attempt to justify uncritical, non-reflective practice based largely on routine responses and guesswork (see the discussions later in this chapter and again in Chapter 7 of 'I prefer to stick to practice'). In the former case, eclecticism refers to a coherent and integrated whole, whereas, in the latter, it has more to do with a messy hotch-potch of unco-ordinated ingredients.

Another problem with methods of intervention is that they are often used in name only. For example, 'I use a task-centred approach' can often simply mean 'I tend to stick to practical tasks', while 'We do a lot of crisis intervention in this team' can sometimes translate as 'We get a lot of short-term emergencies to deal with and we sometimes rush around like headless chickens'. This is not to say that good practice is not possible without using textbook methods, but there is a danger that theoretical labels can be used to disguise the fact that much of the practice undertaken is routine and uncritical, and therefore runs the risk of being dangerous (see Chapter 7).

Heron (2001) provides a helpful way of understanding interventions by dividing them into six categories, as follows:

- *Prescriptive* These interventions involve seeking to direct the behaviour of the person(s) concerned. These are perhaps most closely associated with statutory interventions, for example in enforcing a court order.
- *Informative* The basis of informative interventions is to provide information and/or help people understand their situation or some aspect of it.
- *Confronting* It is sometimes necessary to bring to a client's attention some aspect of their situation that they may not want to face up to. Confronting therefore involves challenging denial and other responses that stand in the way of progress.
- *Cathartic* Catharsis is the process of initiating emotional release, for example by helping someone to express their grief, or by contributing to a warm and safe emotional environment so that people do not feel it is necessary to bottle up their feelings.
- *Catalytic* These interventions are geared towards helping people become more self-directed, more in control of their own lives, in short, a form of empowerment.
- *Supportive* This refers to actions that affirm the value and worth of clients, carers and others involved in the situation.

This is not necessarily a definitive or exhaustive set of categories, but it can be useful as an overview of the range of interventions and a starting point for considering them further.

Ethics and values

In working with other people we enter a complex world of interactions and structures. This can lead to a positive outcome for all concerned or it can lead to a serious exacerbation of the situation. Consequently, we have to recognize the potential for social work to do harm as well as good. This introduces the need for an *ethical* approach, one in which questions of morality and values are taken into consideration.

This does not mean that social workers have to be experts in moral philosophy, but it does mean that we need to be clear about:

- our own values and the ways in which they influence our practice;
- the professional values of social work and how they shape what we can or cannot do;
- the dangers of not taking account of values and the ethical dimension of practice.

This is very complex territory, and so we have to be realistic and accept that the ethical dimension of social work is one that we are likely to continue to wrestle with, rather than one that can be resolved once and for all. An understanding of value issues is therefore an important component of the social work knowledge base, which is why, in this book, they merit a chapter of their own (Chapter 5).

Dialectical reason

This is a philosophical term that refers to the need to understand social and other phenomena in *dynamic* terms. That is, instead of trying to understand the social world in terms of fixed categories or unchanging truths, it is necessary to appreciate that social life is characterized by:

- *Conflict* Conflicting forces and interest groups vie for dominance, and so social life is not entirely stable and based on consensus (see the discussion of consensus vs. conflict models in Chapter 1). For example, people with different perspectives on welfare provision will seek to influence policy and practice so that they become more in line with their own perspective and values (as in the case of political parties).
- *Interaction* Factors in the social world do not sit comfortably side by side – they interact with, and influence, each other. For example,

the market is influenced by the media, but the media are also influenced by the market.

- *Change or flux* Society is constantly changing. Apparent stability is simply a very slow form of change. Where things do remain constant over time, it is because people are working towards maintaining and sustaining them (for example, through rituals and traditional practices).

The main implication of dialectical reason is that we should recognize that the knowledge base of social work is:

- *Contested* There will be competing definitions of what is relevant and what is important. It is not a case of discovering definitive 'truths' that everyone will accept.
- *Interactive* Different elements of the knowledge base will influence each other. For example, although sociological and psychological factors tend to be studied separately, in practice they constantly interact and affect each other.
- *Changing* The knowledge base grows and develops, with new ideas and emphases emerging, while others slip more into the background.

It is for these reasons, amongst others, that social workers need to keep in touch with knowledge base/theoretical issues, so that they can make the best use of the knowledge available.

Using knowledge

Having knowledge is one thing, but being able to use it in actual practice is another. We should not underestimate the skills involved in using knowledge in practice, of integrating theory and practice. In order to use such knowledge we need to be able to:

- *Select* We cannot use all of our knowledge all of the time! Although we will tend to use much of our knowledge without even realizing that we are doing so, we have to be able to decide which aspects of the knowledge base need to be to the fore in any given situation. In order to do this, we need to be clear about what we are trying to achieve so that we can determine which elements of knowledge are relevant, hence the importance of the social work process and systematic practice.

- *Integrate* This applies at two levels. First, there are different strands of knowledge that need to be integrated (psychological, sociological and philosophical knowledge, for example), so that they interweave and inform each other. Second, there is a need to integrate theory and practice, to ensure that formal knowledge is adapted to suit the particular situation being tackled – theory needs to be 'tailored' or made to measure, rather than 'off the peg'.
- *Reflect* It is not enough simply to utilize knowledge and leave it at that. We then need to reflect on our actions and their consequences, so that we can learn from them and adapt our plan of action accordingly. Indeed, the notion of 'reflective practice' is an important one when it comes to using knowledge in practice.

Although not the only issues to consider in using knowledge in practice, these three – select, integrate, reflect – are certainly very important ones. In particular, the third element is worthy of further consideration and so I turn now to an examination of 'reflective practice'.

Reflective practice

The term 'reflective practice' is one closely associated with the educational theorist Donald Schön. Reflective practice involves going beyond the idea of 'fitting the square peg of theory into the round hole of practice':

> Theory cannot be seen as an entity that can simply be taken 'off the shelf' and applied to practice in a mechanistic way. It is better conceived of as an interactive process through which concepts and frameworks are 'made to measure' by the skilful work of the reflective practitioner. ... In this way, human services practice, although based on science, is also very much a craft. (Thompson, 2000b, p. 89)

Reflective practice involves:

- literally 'reflecting' on our practice, before, during and after;
- avoiding routine, blanket approaches that do not consider the specific circumstances in hand;
- avoiding mechanistic, unthinking responses to problems;
- not looking for 'the right answer', as if there is only one possible solution to each problem;

- recognizing that practice situations are generally 'messy', and have to be wrestled with to make sense of them;
- being creative and imaginative, exploring the possible range of solutions;
- 'problem setting' – being clear about what the problem is and how best to respond to it;
- continuous professional development – continuing to learn from practice, constantly improving our knowledge and skills;
- being open to new ideas and other people's perspectives, even if they challenge our own.

The notion of reflecting on practice 'before, during and after' is one worthy of further consideration. Reflection before practice is, of course, planning. It would be unwise to enter into a practice situation without giving at least some thought to the situation that lies ahead. This does not mean that it can be decided in advance how a situation can or should be dealt with – that would be very much against the principles of openness and flexibility associated with reflective practice. However, some degree of forethought can pay dividends – forewarned is, after all, forearmed.

Reflection during practice is what Schön (1983) refers to as 'a reflective conversation with the situation'. That is, there is, or should be, a constant interplay between what is happening and the worker's thoughts and actions. Rather than simply attempting to 'apply' a theory or method mechanistically or impose a particular solution on the situation, the reflective practitioner should keep the situation under constant review, revisiting elements of it and adjusting plans and responses accordingly. Reflection after the event allows us to learn from the experience, to note key aspects of the situation and the part we played in dealing with it, so that we can benefit from the experience in terms of using the insights gained to inform future practice. Reflective practice is discussed further in Chapter 6.

Thoughts and feelings

The discussion so far has concentrated on the 'cognitive' aspects of social work – what we need to know, what thought processes we need to engage with, and so on. However, we should note that there is also the emotional dimension to consider. This applies in two ways:

1. We need to have knowledge and understanding of emotional issues in order to practise effectively. For example, in examining human development, we will need to consider issues related to loss, and the effects that grief and mourning can have on people. Similarly, in examining interpersonal or group interactions, the emotional dimension is likely to be very significant, with the interplay of emotional factors being a major part of interpersonal or group dynamics. We should note that the emotional dimension of social work is concerned not only with the feeling and emotional responses of clients and carers, but also our own. Social workers are human beings dealing often with emotionally demanding situations, and so we should not underplay the importance of understanding how emotional issues apply to us as workers. We are not immune to the pain we encounter in dealing with people's distress.

2. Other aspects of knowledge and learning are significant in emotional terms. For example, in learning about discrimination and oppression, we may have to 'unlearn' a lot of taken-for-granted assumptions, especially where these are based on stereotypes or prejudiced views about particular individuals, groups or aspects of social life. Such unlearning can be painful and frightening at times, and our feelings can sometimes act as a barrier to learning if letting go of certain ideas or assumptions makes us feel insecure.

Our knowledge base, then, should not be seen as something hard and solid, to be distinguished from the softer, more uncertain issues of feelings and emotional responses. The two sets of factors, thinking and feeling, need to be integrated, as they will often influence each other – and indeed, they will both often influence our actions. Consequently, it is imperative that we take on board the emotional dimension of practice in addition to the cognitive elements of knowledge and thought. We need to develop what is often referred to these days as 'emotional intelligence'.

'I prefer to stick to practice'

The comment 'I prefer to stick to practice' is one I have come across a number of times in talking to practitioners about theory–practice issues. The problem with statements like this is that they paint a picture in which theory and practice are entirely separate entities, existing in separate worlds. The reality, of course, is much more complex. Practice cannot be disconnected from ideas, assumptions, frameworks of understanding and so on. Theory and practice are therefore necessarily linked, even if practitioners do not draw on theory openly and explicitly. In effect, the comment 'I prefer to stick to practice' could be interpreted as 'I am not willing to expose my practice to critical scrutiny or to reflect on it'.

The point I am making here is that it is dangerous to ignore, neglect or play down the role of knowledge and theory in underpinning practice. A failure to take seriously the knowledge base can result in a number of problems, not least the following:

- Actions taken may not be in keeping with the law or official policy.
- Inappropriate actions may be taken due to a failure to understand some aspect of the situation.
- Opportunities to take appropriate and helpful actions may be missed due to a lack of awareness of their significance.
- Actions may unwittingly reinforce discrimination and oppression or run counter to other ethical principles.
- Opportunities for learning and professional development are likely to be missed.
- Professional credibility and acceptance in the eyes of others is likely to be more difficult to achieve.
- Opportunities for achieving job satisfaction may be missed.

While recognizing that using knowledge in practice is not always easy or straightforward, these examples of the dangers of neglecting to do so should be sufficient to underline the need to make the necessary effort to make sure that practice owes more to knowledge and reflection than to habit, guesswork or luck.

Conclusion

It should be abundantly clear from this chapter that the overall knowledge base is indeed vast and, what is more, is continuing to develop and change all the time. But, having said this, it is important to stress that practitioners are not realistically expected to know all of this knowledge base, or even most of it – that would simply be too much to ask. For example, we would not expect a geographer, even a very eminent one, to know all that there is to know about the physical and social geography of the Earth. So, what is it realistic to expect from social workers as far as the knowledge base is concerned? My own answer to this question is as follows:

- *An understanding of the basics* Social workers do not have to be experts in the various fields of knowledge, but it *is* realistic to expect them to have at least a grasp of the basics.
- *A willingness to say 'I don't know'* If we do not know everything, then there is no point in pretending that we do. We have to have the humility to be prepared to say 'I don't know'. This is not a sign of weakness or failure, but rather a helpful and constructive recognition of our limitations.
- *Access to further knowledge* While it may be the case that we do not have a particular fact or piece of information immediately at our disposal, this does not mean that we are not expected to make the effort to find out. We therefore need to know what potential sources of information are available to us (managers, experienced colleagues, libraries, the internet and so on) and be prepared to use them.
- *An openness to learning* Sadly, some people seem content to undertake their work in a fairly routine, mechanical way, making use of the knowledge they have, but not being prepared to take the risks involved in being open to further learning. Clearly, this is a dangerous approach to practice, and one that should be replaced with an openness to learning.
- *An ability to be selective* As argued earlier, we cannot use all of our knowledge all of the time, so we have to develop the skills of choosing which elements of the knowledge base are relevant to which aspect of practice.
- *Reflective practice* Knowledge tends to be forgotten if we do not use it; it slips into the background and often disappears altogether. It is therefore important that we reflect on our practice so that we continue to draw on that knowledge base and keep it alive and of value.

The prospect of using this immense and changing knowledge base in practice may seem quite daunting at first. However, it is something that, with experience and a commitment to developing the necessary skills, can become not only a major contribution to good practice, but also a great source of interest, enjoyment and job satisfaction.

Guide to further learning

There are a number of books that address human development (for example, Durkin, 1995) although many focus particularly on child development (Barnes, 1995; Davenport, 1994; Oates, 1994; see also Thompson, 2002b). The classic work on the subject is Erikson (1980), although this does tend to lack awareness of broader social issues (the significance of gender, for example). Wheal (1998) provides a practical guide to working with people going through adolescence. Robinson (1995) provides a good critique of approaches that fail to deal adequately with issues of race and culture.

There is also a wealth of literature available on the general subject of social processes and institutions. The two I prefer personally are Giddens (2001) and Abercrombie *et al.* (2000), although there are many other good books available. In considering the more specific issues of how these factors affect social work, Thompson (2001) and Thompson (2003a) both address these issues at length.

Interpersonal interactions are well covered in Egan (1977), Egan (1998) and Johnson (1993), and also feature in Thompson (2002a). Communication and language issues are given extensive treatment in Thompson (2003b). Group interactions can be studied further in Baron *et al.* (1992) and various works by Tom Douglas. See also Doel and Sawdon (1999) for a very helpful overview. Organizational issues are covered thoroughly in Mullins (1996) and, with specific reference to social work, are addressed in Chapter 6 of Thompson (2003a).

The social work process is covered in Chapters 19 to 23 of Thompson (2002a). Egan (1998), although not directly concerned with social work, is also a helpful source. The theory and practice of evaluation are well covered in Shaw (1996).

Theoretical paradigms and methods of intervention are discussed in some depth in Payne (1997) while Stepney and Ford (2000) provide a helpful overview. Dialectical reason is discussed in Thompson (2000b) and Thompson (2003a).

Emotional intelligence is covered in Goleman (1996) and Merlevede *et al.* (2001), although both books share the characteristic so often found in writings on this subject, namely a tendency to overemphasize the biological dimension at the expense of psychological and social dimensions.

The question of using knowledge in practice and the related concept of reflective practice are discussed in Thompson (2000b) and Thompson and Bates (1996). Palmer *et al.* (1994), although written from a nursing perspective, is a very useful source book on reflective practice. Martyn (2000) and Fook *et al.* (2000) are also both useful texts.

Exercise 3

Consider a piece of social work intervention (placing a child with foster carers, assessing an older person's needs or writing a report for court, for example). What elements of knowledge would be relevant to the situation you have chosen? What would you need to know? There are no 'right' answers to this. It is simply an exercise to get you thinking about the knowledge base. Use the space below to make some notes.

4

The skills base

Introduction

It was emphasized in Chapter 3 that the knowledge base, although very important indeed, does not give us ready-made answers as to how we should proceed in a given situation. Part of the art of the social worker is choosing the most appropriate response to the situation in hand. The knowledge base will be very useful in giving us lots of insights and clues about the situations we face, but it is still down to us to develop the necessary skills for effective practice. The knowledge base therefore needs to be supplemented by a *skills* base. And, once again, we shall see that the territory we need to explore is complex, multifaceted and constantly changing. So, the skills base lays before us another set of challenges.

This chapter outlines the range of skills involved in high-quality social work and considers what is involved in the process of skill development. I begin, though, by exploring the notion of 'competences' and the six key tasks identified in the National Occupational Standards for Social Work.

Competent to practise

In 1996, CCETSW, the body responsible for establishing the Diploma in Social Work, the qualification which preceded the current degree in social work, published a document which indicated what we should be able to expect from a newly qualified social worker in terms of skills and competences. This document set out the details of the 'competences' social work students need to demonstrate while on placement in order to establish that they are 'fit to practise'. The term 'competence' refers to a demonstrable ability to fulfil one or more aspects of the role, and is therefore closely linked to the notion of skill.

CCETSW (1996) identified six of these. I shall explore each of these in turn before considering the National Occupational Standards and the Code of Practice for Social Care Workers.

Communicate and engage

Being able to get your message across clearly and effectively is, of course, a basic element of effective practice, whether we are referring to spoken or written communications. Being sensitive to what others are trying to convey to us is, of course, just as important. This competence involves being able to communicate effectively with:

- clients, carers and other members of the community;
- people within one's own organization in order to make best use of the resources, facilities and support available;
- colleagues in other organizations in the public, private and voluntary sectors in order to develop, consolidate and benefit from multidisciplinary networks.

However, we should not forget about the word 'engage', as this is not simply a synonym for 'communicate'. To engage implies being able to enter into an effective working relationship based on a degree of trust and respect (note a *degree* of trust and respect – it would be unrealistic to expect more than this in many cases). Although good communication is certainly a key part of engagement, it is possible to communicate very well indeed, but still not succeed in engaging. For example, a social worker may convey information very clearly to a client, listen carefully to the responses given, but still not gain the trust of that client, perhaps because the communication was too 'clinical' or unfeeling. This may indicate a failure in terms of handling feelings or sensitivity and observation skills (see below). Engagement, then, is the basis of partnership.

Promote and enable

CCETSW (1996) describe this competence in the following terms: 'Promote opportunities for people to use their own strengths and expertise to enable them to meet their responsibilities, secure rights and achieve change' (p. 11). This description implies a number of important points:

- *A focus on strengths* Social workers are, in a way, professional problem solvers, and so one danger is the tendency to focus on problems and negatives, perhaps at the expense of considering the strengths and positives of the person and situation. It is therefore important to remember to focus on strengths as well as weaknesses.
- *People's own expertise* The social worker brings a degree of expertise to each situation, but so too do clients and carers. Working in partnership involves recognizing and building on that expertise, rather than creating a pseudo-medical relationship where the social worker is the expert who 'diagnoses' the problem and 'prescribes' the cure.
- *Meeting responsibilities and securing rights* The question of helping clients to fulfil their responsibilities is a major one in social work (for example, in relation to parental responsibilities in child-care cases), but the question of helping people secure their rights is one that tends to receive far less attention.
- *Achieving change* Helping to meet needs and solve problems necessarily involves bringing about change in the particular situations encountered. Promoting opportunities to bring about positive change is therefore an important social work activity.

Assess and plan

A central part of the social worker's role, as we saw in Chapter 3, is to assess and plan. This means gathering information to form a picture of the key elements of the situation, the strengths and weaknesses, the steps that have to be taken to resolve the situation and so on. This has to be done in partnership so that the plans developed are shared, thereby increasing the likelihood that they will be successful as a result of the joint commitment on which the partnership is based.

Achieving success in assessing and planning involves:

- the ability to gather relevant information without being over-intrusive and infringing people's civil liberties;
- forming a picture, jointly with the other relevant parties, of the key issues so that a plan of action can be formulated;
- agreeing a way forward to meet the identified needs or resolve the identified problems;
- monitoring and reviewing the situation in order to respond appropriately to changes and developments, as and when they occur.

The competence of 'assess and plan' is therefore quite a complex and demanding one, involving a range of skills such as communication, analysis, negotiation, co-ordination, and so on.

Intervene and provide services

Assessment is, of course, the precursor to intervention, in the sense that how, when and whether we intervene, what services we provide or organize will depend to a very large extent on the outcome of the assessment and the plans drawn up as a result of it. Being able to identify the steps that need to be taken is one thing, being able to take them is another – involving another set of skills. This involves:

- a range of problem-solving activities geared towards empowering people – so that they are in a better position to deal with their own problems;
- providing/commissioning and managing a package of care-related services or other supportive measures;
- supporting people through the process of change;
- contributing to the management of risk; and so on.

Much of this work depends on effective communication and engagement skills, as discussed above. However, there are also a number of other skills involved, including several of those outlined below. The whole area of intervening and providing services is vast in its scope, covering a range of activities across a number of client groups and scenarios. It is not surprising, then, that so much skill and expertise is involved.

Work in organizations

Of course, social workers do not operate independently of their employing organization. It is therefore necessary to develop the ability to work effectively within that organization by:

- playing a part in the planning, monitoring and control of resources so that they are used to the best effect;
- working as an accountable professional within the context of agency policies and procedures;
- contributing to wider organizational processes, such as the evaluation of the impact and appropriateness of policies and practices within the agency.

This is an important part of being a professional, as it involves going beyond being simply an employee who follows instructions and may have little commitment to the organization's aims. An accountable professional is one who takes responsibility for doing whatever is reasonably possible to pursue professional aims, and this includes making a positive contribution towards influencing the organization in order to maximize the potential for achieving those aims (see the discussion of the 'organizational operator' in Thompson, 2003a).

This can be a demanding task, particularly in some organizations where there is a lot of conflict, or where the aims and purpose of the organization's activities have become lost in the confusion of day-to-day pressures (see Chapter 7). It is therefore important that people work together to support each other in their efforts.

Develop professional competence

One expectation of professional practice is that practitioners continue to learn and develop. That is, it is not enough simply to focus on learning until a professional qualification has been achieved, and then 'coast in neutral' without devoting a lot of time, effort and energy to further learning, or – to use the technical term – 'continuous professional development' (CPD). This involves:

- using information sources appropriately;
- reflecting upon and critically evaluating one's own practice;
- being flexible and responsive;
- contributing to 'the resolution of professional dilemmas and conflicts, balancing rights, needs and perspectives' (CCETSW, 1996, p. 12); and
- making use of learning opportunities through supervision, training, appraisal and so on.

The extent to which CPD is encouraged for practitioners will depend to a large extent on the organization concerned. This is because there is considerable variation between organizations in terms of the extent to which they support and facilitate learning. This is not simply a matter of the size of the training budget, but rather, relates to a whole range of issues connected to the organization's culture, values and commitment to its staff.

Expectations of practice

What counts as an acceptable level of practice has been a matter of considerable debate for a very long time. However, in recent years there have been concerted efforts to pin down agreed standards of practice. These efforts have produced two important outcomes, the National Occupational Standards for Social Work and the Code of Practice for Social Care Workers (see the 'Guide to further learning' for details of how to obtain these documents).

The National Occupational Standards identify six key roles:

1. Prepare for, and work with, individuals, families, carers, groups and communities to assess their needs and circumstances.
2. Plan, carry out, review and evaluate social work practice, with individuals, families, carers, groups, communities and other professionals.
3. Support individuals to represent their needs, views and circumstances and to achieve greater independence.
4. Manage risk to individuals, families, carers, groups, communities, self and colleagues.
5. Manage and be accountable, with supervision and support, for their own social work practice within their organization.
6. Demonstrate and be responsible for professional competence in social work practice.

In tandem with these six key roles, the Code of Practice for Social Care Workers establishes that social care workers (including social workers) must:

1. Protect the rights and promote the interests of service users and carers.
2. Strive to establish and maintain the trust and confidence of service users and carers.
3. Promote the independence of service users while protecting them as far as possible from danger or harm.
4. Respect the rights of service users whilst seeking to ensure that their behaviour does not harm themselves or other people.
5. Uphold public trust and confidence in social care services.
6. Be accountable for the quality of their work and take responsibility for maintaining and improving their knowledge and skills.

Clearly, these two documents add up to an expectation of a wide range of skills. While the six core competences identified above will go some considerable way towards meeting these skill requirements, they will not cover all that is required. We therefore need to consider what other skills are required. First, though, we need to be clear about what we mean by a skill.

What is a skill?

Whereas the competences outlined above are fairly broad, skills can be seen to be much narrower and more specific. A skill is the ability to carry out a particular activity effectively and consistently over a period of time. Skills are characterized by the fact that they can be *learned*. This is an important point, as it allows us to realize that a number of things that are generally regarded as 'qualities' or relatively fixed parts of our personality are in fact skills, in so far as they can be learned over time. Examples would include:

- *Patience* Being patient is something that can be learned through practice and the development of the ability to stay calm and in control. This can be achieved simply through practice over a period of time or by the use of specific techniques (breathing control methods, for example).
- *Sensitivity* Similarly, the skill of being sensitive and tactful is one that can be 'worked on', so that the tendency to 'put our foot in it' can be lessened or removed altogether.
- *Being well organized* A common comment from people is that of 'I'm not a well-organized person', as if this were some fixed and immutable part of their life, rather than an area of skill development yet to be tackled. Systems for being better organized can be learned, and the myth that disorganization is inevitable for some people can be rejected.
- *Confidence* Confidence is linked to self-esteem, the value that we attach to ourselves. Again, we can learn how to appreciate our strengths and learn how to benefit from a more confident approach.

Different people begin at different starting points in terms of skill development, and so some people have more ground to cover than others. But this is not to say that those that are in the early stages of developing a particular skill cannot or will not develop that skill in due course. I shall return to the question of developing skills below, but the important point to emphasize here is that skills are not something you either have or not – they can be developed and nurtured.

What skills do social workers need?

A lot, is the short answer! However, to get things into perspective we should first of all recognize that most if not all people coming into the social work profession already have a good basis in many of the relevant skills – communication, co-ordination, creativity and so on. Skill development in social work education therefore tends to involve two main elements:

1. building on, consolidating, enhancing and sharpening existing skills; and
2. recognizing, understanding and developing new skills.

For the sake of clarity I have divided up the basic skills, as I see them, into 15 categories. These are not mutually exclusive, as some skills will inevitably fall into more than one category. The list of skills outlined should also not be seen as comprehensive or exhaustive – it would probably take an encyclopaedia to detail all the skills that a social worker can potentially draw upon in the course of his or her duties.

Communication skills

Communication has already been identified as a key component of the skills base by virtue of its inclusion in the six core competences. It is because of its central role in social work that it is worth now revisiting the theme of communication and exploring it in more detail.

Communication, it must be acknowledged, comes in many forms, and can be categorized as follows:

- *Verbal* This refers to face-to-face interactions and involves the impact of the actual words we use in speaking, the way they are constructed into sentences, the way they are pronounced or emphasized, and so on. Social workers have to learn how to tailor what they are saying to the specific context in which it is being said, for example in terms of the level of formality. Formal speech when it is not called for can cause unnecessary barriers, and informal speech when formal speech is required (in court, for example) can also cause problems.

- *Telephone* In some respects, this is a sub-division of verbal com- munication, but has the added dimension of not being able to see the other person, and so, in some ways, is actually more difficult than direct verbal communication. Having a good telephone manner is therefore an important part of the social worker's repertoire. An abrupt or otherwise inappropriate telephone manner can cause a great deal of ill-feeling and therefore act as a barrier to effective communication.

- *Non-verbal* Verbal communication is usually accompanied by a range of other signals, commonly known as 'body language'. These can be very powerful signals and, where there is a clash or conflict between what is said verbally and what is said non-verbally, we tend to attach more credence to the latter. Non-verbal communication is often an indicator of emotional state or mood. Social workers need to be able to 'read' it successfully, as well as use their own body language to good effect.

- *Writing* Communicating in writing is also a very skilled activity, and it is one that social workers find themselves having to use quite a lot. A great deal depends on the written word in terms of reports, agency records, letters and so on. An ability to communicate very well indeed at a verbal level will not compensate for an inability to communicate effectively in writing.

Social workers therefore need to be able to develop and consolidate a range of communication skills so that they are able to make a success of the interpersonal interactions that are often at the heart of social work practice.

One important point to recognize is that communication is a two-way process, and therefore involves listening as well as speaking (or writing). That is, we need to be able to get our message across but also be very receptive to the messages that other people are giving us. Sometimes we can become so swallowed up in what we are trying to say to someone that we do not devote enough attention to listening to what he or she is trying to say to us. We have to make sure that we work very hard to keep the channels of communication open.

Communication is a complex issue, not least because of the factors that affect it. For example, patterns of communication are not uni- versal and tend to vary across cultures, genders, age groups, classes and other dimensions of the social world. Indeed, given that lan- guage is so socially significant, it should come as no surprise to find that communication has much to do with social factors. The lessons that social workers learn about power, social divisions and social location therefore also have to be applied to communication.

An increasingly important aspect of communication that is worthy of comment is the use of information and communication technology (ICT), through faxes, computers, the internet and so on. Unfortunately, there appears to be a considerable degree of 'technophobia' in social work (Bates, 1995), with many practitioners being unwilling or at least reluctant to make use of the developments in technology in recent years. This is a great pity, as ICT offers considerable scope in terms of communication, information gathering and research.

An additional skill in relation to communication is what I call 'communicative sensitivity' (Thompson, 2003b). This refers to not only being able to communicate, but also being able to recognize when we need to communicate, with whom and so on. There is little use in having excellent communication skills if we do not have the sensitivity to work out when we need to use them. The problem is often not so much *poor* communication as *a lack of* communication.

Self-awareness skills

In social work an important component of what goes on, and an important resource to draw upon, is the worker him- or herself. That is, much of what we have to offer comes from our own personality or our own personal resources, hence the commonly used term, 'use of self'. As we are, in effect, a tool of intervention in our own right, it clearly pays dividends to have some degree of understanding of that tool or resource.

At its simplest level, self-awareness involves having at least some notion of how other people perceive us, how we come across to them. First impressions are, of course, important, but so too are second and third impressions. We are constantly giving people a picture of who we are and what we are like. We therefore have to ask: What impression do other people have of me? Is it the same impression that I have of myself?

Often, the same characteristic may be viewed differently by other people. For example, consider the following pairings in terms of how the same behaviour can be viewed differently:

relaxed and friendly	vs.	overfamiliar
strong and assertive	vs.	pushy or bossy
laid-back	vs.	uncaring
quietly confident	vs.	timid or shy

concerned	vs.	nosey
cheerful	vs.	flippant
a good listener	vs.	passive or lazy
keen to help	vs.	paternalistic

Clearly there are problems associated with continuing to hold views of yourself in line with those on the left-hand side, while others may be more inclined to agree with the comments on the right. It is therefore necessary to gain feedback from others in terms of how they react to you (is their response to you consistent with your image of yourself, or is there something you can learn from this?). Supervision, training and peer support are all further ways in which this aspect of self-awareness can be explored and developed.

The other side of self-awareness, though, is that of developing an understanding of how external factors affect you. Often, we can be affected by a situation without realizing straight away what impact it has had on us. For example, we can sometimes be irritated by a situation but, because the irritation has developed slowly, we may not notice that we are giving off signals about how we feel (for example, through tone of voice). Similarly, we may become steadily depressed about something, and it is only when someone else points it out to us that we realize that we have slipped into a depressed state of mind. Consequently, it is important that we develop the skills of 'keeping in touch' with our feelings. This notion has become something of a cliché in social work, but it none the less has more than a grain of truth in it. Social work can be very emotionally demanding at times, so we have to make sure that we do not neglect the feelings dimension of our work (see Handling feelings below).

Self-awareness is something that can develop over time. But note, however, that it does not automatically do so. Indeed, the longer we go without considering what effect other people and situations are having on us, the more ingrained and fixed our view can become – and thus potentially more out of touch with reality. Also, the longer we go without reflecting on such issues, the more uncomfortable or threatening it can be to do so. It therefore pays to develop this habit from an early stage in one's career and continue to keep a clear focus on how we are affecting other people and how they are affecting us.

Analytical skills

In the field of management studies, the topic of analytical skills is given a lot of attention, but sadly their significance in social work is not always fully realized. The ability to analyse involves breaking a situation or issue down into its component parts so that the inter-connections and patterns can be uncovered. This can be seen to consist of the following elements:

- identifying the key issues within a particular situation, sorting out the important 'bits' from a mass of information;
- recognizing patterns across a range of factors, noticing intercon-nections;
- understanding the processes that feed into the situation and flow from it (inputs and outputs).

These skills are developed and tested through the academic com-ponents of the course. In this respect, the skills of, for example, essay writing are also practice skills, in the sense that both academic study and social work practice rely on analytical skills.

These skills are used in a number of ways in the context of actual practice, as the following examples illustrate:

- *Planning* Formulating a plan of intervention necessarily involves analysing past events, current circumstances and likely future trends so that decisions can be made about how best to proceed.
- *Assessment* In effect, assessment is in itself a form of analysis, involving, as it does, the gathering and sifting of information and the identification of key issues to address.
- *Review* The process of review involves analysing what has hap-pened since the initial assessment and amending or confirming the plan of action, as appropriate.
- *Evaluation* Learning the lessons from our practice entails analys-ing what happened, what worked well (and why) and what could have been done better.
- *Problem solving* Problem solving is a creative, rather than mech-anical, process, and so it involves analysing the current situation and generating a range of possible solutions or ways forward so that these too can be analysed, and the most appropriate one adopted.
- *Setting priorities* As argued in Chapter 1, social work necessarily involves setting priorities due to the fact that demand is always likely to exceed supply. Deciding which issues are the most impor-tant or pressing once again involves a process of analysis.

Analytical skills can take time to develop, but can be encouraged by asking the following three questions in relation to the situation being considered:

1. What patterns can be detected here?
2. What appear to be the most important elements in this situation?
3. What appear to be the important connections or inter-relationships?

These will not provide everything you need to know, but should provide you with a good starting point.

Handling feelings

The point has already been made that social work is a professional activity with a significant emotional component. This is partly because the work involves dealing with people who are experiencing distress, disadvantage and discrimination and other related difficulties, and partly because the work involves processes of change, often painful change, for example, in coming to terms with a loss or responding to a crisis.

As with self-awareness, there are two sides to this. First, we need to consider the significance of emotional issues for clients, carers and other significant people we deal with. This involves developing sensitivity and observation skills so that we are able to recognize the 'emotional signals' that people give off, but also involves understanding how emotions work and their role in human psychology. For example, we should realize that there is little point in trying to brush emotional issues under the carpet, as if they will go away if we ignore them. Indeed, they are much more likely to resurface elsewhere, possibly in another form, and possibly in negative or destructive ways. For example, if intense anger is not acknowledged, it may emerge later as depression.

Recognizing and responding appropriately to the feelings dimension is an important part of professional practice for a number of reasons, including the following:

- Intense emotions can prevent people from thinking or acting rationally. To ignore the emotional dimension is therefore to ignore what could be a crucial element in making sense of the situation.
- Emotions can sometimes 'paralyse' people, as they get stuck in a situation which is too painful or distressing to deal with. This can easily be mistaken for a lack of co-operation.
- If people feel their feelings are not being taken into account, they are unlikely to have a great deal of respect for, or confidence in, the worker.

- Emotional responses to situations can manifest themselves as aggression and violence, sometimes directed towards the worker.
- Sometimes people can be so overwhelmed by emotions that they feel as though they have 'nothing to lose' and can therefore behave in very self-destructive ways (for example, through suicidal behaviours).

The other side of the emotional dimension is, of course, being able to handle our own feelings. Social work takes its toll of everyone that is involved in it, although its demands can usually be kept within manageable limits (see the discussion of stress in Chapter 7). It is both naïve and dangerous, then, to ignore the emotional impact of the work on the worker. This does not mean that we have to engage in a lengthy process of emotional introspection every time we complete a social work task, but it does mean that we have to be sensitive to the ways in which our work affects us so that we can:

- recognize the influence of our own feelings on particular situations, for example where anger may be affecting our judgement;
- use our emotions constructively where possible – for example, as a source of motivation;
- seek support where necessary (for example, through supervision or 'debriefing') to avoid levels of pressure becoming harmful and stressful.

Self-management skills

In my book on *People Skills* I made the point that:

> The skills involved in maximizing personal effectiveness can be seen to be very important because they underpin all the other skills involved in working with people. That is, if we are not able to manage ourselves, we will be in a much weaker position in terms of managing situations involving other people. For example, if I do not manage my time very well, then I will be left with less time and energy to work effectively with service users and colleagues. Good people skills have their roots in personal effectiveness. (Thompson, 2002a, p. 1)

There are many such personal effectiveness or 'self-management' skills but, for present purposes, I shall focus on three in particular:

- *Assertiveness* This involves maintaining the balance between the two unhelpful extremes of being aggressive (trying to bully other people into doing what you want them to do) and being submissive or 'non-assertive' (allowing other people to bully you into what they want you to do). Being assertive means striking a balance between these two extremes, enabling both parties to interact constructively and both to achieve their aims. This involves being able to communicate and negotiate effectively and is therefore a very skilled activity that needs to be developed over time.

- *Stress management*   Social work is a pressurized activity. That is, it involves being exposed to a range of demands and pressures. However, there are steps that can be taken to help prevent these pressures spilling over into harmful, health-affecting stress. This includes monitoring our own levels of pressure, developing our coping abilities and being willing to seek out support when we need it (seeing asking for help as a sign of strength, rather than weakness).

- *Time management*   There is only so much time (and energy) available for undertaking our work. These scarce resources therefore have to be managed as effectively as possible so that time is not wasted and energy is not dissipated unnecessarily. Consequently, there is much to be gained from being clear about how best to use the time and personal resources available to us.

Self-management or personal effectiveness skills have not always received the attention they deserve in social work education, and so there are still many experienced practitioners who may not appreciate their significance or may not have had the opportunity to learn how to develop them. However, the fact that some practitioners may struggle with this aspect of practice does not, of course, diminish the importance of such skills in any way (these skills are discussed further in Chapter 7).

Presentation skills

In a way, the question of presentation skills follows on from the earlier discussion of communication skills. However, I include it as a category in its own right, as I feel that it refers to a set of skills that are often neglected, with many practitioners feeling they have had little or no training in presenting a verbal report at a case conference or a large meeting or giving evidence in court.

Presentation skills are needed because the social worker often acts as a focal point or fulcrum of a multidisciplinary network. In this role, he or she needs to be able to present information clearly and effectively to groups of people. Although this can be quite anxiety provoking for many social workers, it is none the less often a necessary part of the role. It is important, then, to be clear about what is involved in making an effective presentation. The basic elements can be summarized as follows:

- *Be prepared* Be clear about what you are going to say and why *before* you are called upon to speak. It is not necessary to have a prepared speech to be read out word for word, but some advance planning generally pays dividends, not least in keeping anxiety levels down.
- *Be clear about the purpose* It is important to remember *why* you are making a presentation, as the purpose of the presentation should be a major influence on what is said and how. For example, deciding what to include and what to leave out will depend to a large extent on the purpose of making the presentation in the first place.
- *Get the balance right* This means avoiding the extremes of saying too much and saying too little. Waffling will not endear you to those present, and neither will giving people only a very sketchy picture that does not really help them to make sense of the situation. Again, this balance will depend, to a certain extent at least, on the purpose of the presentation.
- *Get the tone right* The balance of what to say also needs to be matched by the balance of how to say it, especially in terms of how formal you should be. If you are too formal, you can create barriers, but if, by contrast, you are too informal, it can appear that you are too casual, not taking things seriously enough.
- *Relax!* This is, of course, more easily said than done, but the fact remains that one of the biggest obstacles to effective presentations is our own anxiety. If we are not careful, we can create a self-fulfilling prophecy in which worrying about getting it wrong actually contributes to our getting it wrong!

It can take a long time to become proficient at making presentations well, and so we should not expect to become very competent overnight. A lot of patience is needed, along with a willingness to learn from mistakes and to carry on learning.

Co-ordination skills

Effective co-ordination is part of the process of time management discussed above, but there are also other aspects of co-ordination that are worthy of comment. I shall comment on three in particular:

1. *Care management*   Social workers are often involved in the process of care management. This means co-ordinating a package of care-related measures for an individual or family in need of community care services, as identified by an assessment carried out under the NHS and Community Care Act 1990. This involves a number of skills in terms of being able to co-ordinate the involvement of various people (care providers, GPs, financial administrators, and so on), to monitor the process, review its effectiveness and appropriateness and intervene where necessary. Being an effective care manager therefore involves being well organized to at least a basic level of proficiency.

2. *Multidisciplinary work*   Many forms of social work are directly multidisciplinary in nature, for example in child protection services or community mental health teams. However, it could be argued that all forms of social work are at least indirectly multidisciplinary, in so far as there is a need to liaise with one or more professional groups as part of the social work process, from assessment, through intervention and review, to termination and evaluation. Maintaining good links with a wide range of groups, particularly where some may have different priorities and/or values from our own, can be a highly skilled undertaking.

3. *Workload management*   Social work is, as we noted in Chapter 1, characterized by situations where demand exceeds supply. Workers therefore have to be careful that they do not overload themselves with work to the point where they are not functioning properly, or where they are experiencing stress. Consequently, the skills of being able to manage and co-ordinate a heavy workload are very valuable ones in social work. Co-ordination skills therefore include the ability to co-ordinate oneself in terms of setting priorities and so on.

One of the basic elements of co-ordination is the ability to 'get the big picture', or what is sometimes referred to as 'helicopter vision' – the ability to rise above a situation and get an overview before descending into the situation to deal with it. This ability to get an overview and see the interconnections between the various elements is a fundamental part of co-ordination, and is therefore an ability well worth cultivating.

It should also be apparent that the process of co-ordination is closely associated with communication skills. To be able to co-ordinate with various groups of people involves being not only well organized but also proficient in communicating effectively and appropriately with different people in different settings. This is one example, then, of the ways in which sets of skills need to be seen as part of a greater whole, rather than as isolated matters in their own right.

Sensitivity and observation skills

Sensitivity is an ambiguous word, but I would argue that it is relevant to social work in both ways. First, it can be used as a slightly derogatory term, to refer to someone being 'touchy' (thereby implying that they are being oversensitive). It is important that social workers manage to avoid this type of sensitivity, that they do not overreact to situations, especially when so many aspects of social work can be very highly charged emotionally. Second, it can refer to the much more positive process of being a keen observer, being sensitive to the nuances of the situations you are involved in. It is in this latter sense that sensitivity is an important ability to develop.

Two central aspects of sensitivity can be readily identified:

1. *Reading body language* Non-verbal communication is a very powerful medium for conveying feelings. Developing sensitivity to what is going on in a particular scenario will therefore depend on the ability to 'read' body language. Ironically, one barrier to developing such skills is that we are already quite skilled in such matters, simply as a result of our upbringing in a social world. That is, we can be so used to reading body language that we do not appreciate what is involved and may therefore struggle to improve on it. A careful study of non-verbal communication can therefore be useful in sensitizing us to the subtle and complex ways in which 'signals' are 'transmitted' through the intricate workings of body language.
2. *Empathy* Sympathy involves sharing the same feeling with one or more people. Empathy is similar but subtly and importantly different. Empathy involves understanding or appreciating the feelings of others, but without necessarily experiencing them. This is an important ability in social work, in so far as each day we encounter a range of often intense feelings. We have to be sensitive to those feelings if we are to practise effectively, but we would soon be overwhelmed (and therefore of little use) if we were actually to share those feelings. There is therefore a fundamental skill (or set of skills) in being able to achieve empathy without this becoming sympathy. This is not to say that we should never share feelings with clients or others – that would be naïve and unrealistic – but we

none the less have to be careful not to allow ourselves to become overloaded emotionally.

In addition to these two central themes, there are several other important issues to consider, including the following:

- *Interpersonal dynamics* Body language often follows distinct patterns, reflecting the interpersonal dynamics that are part and parcel of social life – the to-ing and fro-ing of interactions between individuals and groups.
- *Power relations* One person seeking permission from another before speaking, or one or more persons being excluded are examples of how power relations can manifest themselves in family or group situations.
- *The 'light in the fridge' paradox* How do we know what effect our own presence is having? We need to be sensitive to our own part in each particular situation we deal with.
- *Crisis points* Sometimes people's behaviour, attitudes or levels of motivation change significantly because they have reached a crisis or turning point in their lives. Understanding the significance of crisis as a factor in human psychology is therefore an important part of developing sensitivity.
- *Awareness of difference* A person's social background (in terms of class, ethnicity, gender and so on) will be a significant factor in shaping responses to situations. Consequently, we need to take account of such issues in 'reading' the situations we are dealing with.

Reflection skills

The value of reflective practice has already been emphasized. Being able to learn from our practice is, in many ways, a precursor to the development of the other skills outlined here, and so the habit of reflecting on our practice is one that is well worth developing. This is because, while skills can develop spontaneously, they are likely to develop faster and more fully if deliberate efforts are made to learn from experience. And this is where reflective practice comes in.

As we saw in Chapter 2, reflective practice involves avoiding un-critical, routinized practice by remaining open to new ideas, new perspectives and new approaches. There is no easy or short-term route to achieving these abilities, but they can be facilitated over a period of time through various strategies, including the following:

- frequent reviews of practice – not losing sight of the objectives identified and the agreed plan of action for achieving them;
- using opportunities for formal supervision and appraisal – making use of the perspective that line managers and others can bring through formal support systems;
- using informal peer supervision and support – drawing on the insights, feedback and differences of perspective that colleagues can provide;
- undertaking in-service training as and when appropriate – using the learning opportunities that are provided through staff development activities;
- contributing to 'practice teaching' – that is, acting as a supervisor of students on placement, or assisting more experienced colleagues in doing so;
- evaluating practice – for example, by inviting feedback from clients.

Reflection is also closely associated with emancipatory practice, in the sense that discrimination and oppression are often so deeply ingrained that we tend not to notice them much of the time. Consequently, practice based on uncritical routines can easily reinforce patterns of inequality and disadvantage. Reflection skills are important, then, in promoting not only continuous learning and professional development but also equality and social justice.

Creativity

Part of reflective practice, as we have seen, is the avoidance of the 'tramlines' that can so easily lead us into routinized, mechanical practice. Developing the skills involved in creativity is therefore an important contribution to good practice. It is therefore worth considering what is involved in creativity and how this can be developed.

We have to rely on habits and routines up to a point – we would really struggle to deal with our day-to-day demands if we had to 'reinvent the wheel' every time we tried to move forward. However, creativity tends to suffer when we rely too heavily on such habits and routines – our ability to think and act creatively can be stifled by over-restrictive habits. A major part of developing creativity, then, is to break free of such routines, and to look at situations from a different perspective. If we do not make the effort to do this, we run the risk of:

- following patterns uncritically and therefore responding inappropriately to situations that do not fit into the mainstream;
- failing to appreciate significant differences between situations because we concentrate too heavily on what they have in common;
- reinforcing inequality and disadvantage by forcing diverse people and patterns into standardized 'tramlines';
- missing out on opportunities for learning and job satisfaction.

The strategies outlined above in relation to reflective skills can also have a part to play in developing creativity. In addition, it is also worth noting that there is a range of other techniques that can be drawn upon to encourage creative approaches (see, for example, Chapter 24 of Thompson, 2002a). However, although specific techniques can be very useful indeed, we should not rely too heavily on them, as this can lead us full circle back to uncritical routines if we are not careful. We should therefore remain open to new possibilities in whatever ways we reasonably can.

Creativity is also not simply a psychological process – it can and should be a collective endeavour, for example by people working together to 'bounce ideas off each other'. In this way, we can stimulate creativity in each other. Nor should creativity be seen as the preserve of the professionals. If partnership is to be more than empty rhetoric, we should be working with clients and carers in order to encourage and facilitate creativity, with all parties contributing towards breaking down the restrictive barriers of habit and routine.

It is also worth noting that creativity can be linked with confidence and security. The more confident we are, and the more secure we feel about our abilities, the more likely we are to think and act creatively. Although necessity can indeed be the mother of invention, confidence and security also have an important part to play.

Thinking on your feet

For many aspects of social work there is scope for careful and deliberate planning, with no need to rush about. However, at times, there is a need for a very quick response. Situations can arise where it is necessary to 'think on our feet', to be able to react quickly but without panicking. Indeed, this is the crux of the matter – *do not panic!* When a highly pressurized situation develops, there may be little or no time to plan a measured response, but we none the less have to respond calmly without losing our grip. The danger of acting rashly in pressurized situations is therefore one we have to be wary of.

How, then, should we handle such situations where we need to think on our feet? What steps can we take to minimize the risk of panicking? Once again, there are no simple, formula answers to these questions, but the following pointers should be of some value at least:

- *Anticipate* Difficult situations can often be anticipated if we are sensitive to some of the tell-tale signs that all is not well.
- *Keep the channels of communication open* Some tense situations can lead to a tendency to cease communication, perhaps at the moment when it is needed most.
- *Acknowledge feelings* This can help to defuse difficult situations, and is also an important part of effective practice in its own right (see Handling feelings above).
- *Get an overview of the situation* Sometimes we can react hurriedly to one aspect of the circumstances we encounter, with the result that it has a detrimental effect on other aspects of the situation. To try and get the 'big picture', although difficult in pressurized circumstances, can be a big help.
- *Keep calm* Asking people to relax or keep calm is often an effective way of winding them up! However, we should take whatever steps we can to stop the situation from 'boiling over'. This can be through appropriate body language and tone of voice – calming others can have the effect of calming oneself.
- *Keep a clear focus* A tense or difficult situation can lead us to adopt 'survival' behaviours and, in the process, lose sight of why we are there – thereby losing track of what we are trying to do or how we should go about it.

Humility

Humility is the 'quality or state of being humble in spirit: freedom from pride or arrogance' (Webster's *Third New International Dictionary*). I would go a step further in stating that it is the skill of being able to recognize the limitations of what can be achieved in difficult and constraining circumstances whilst remaining positive and constructive. That is, I see humility as the ability to achieve a balance between the two destructive extremes of arrogance and complacency on the one hand and defeatism and cynicism on the other. In this sense, it can be seen as a form of realism, bringing a sense of perspective to our work.

In this respect, humility would be characterized by:

- not having unrealistic expectations about what can be achieved;
- recognizing our limitations and therefore not having an inflated view of our capabilities;
- acknowledging the enormity of the social work task in seeking to address personal and social problems;
- understanding that new challenges can arise at any moment;
- recognizing that we regularly run the risk of making errors – we are not immune to mistakes.

I have previously discussed humility in relation to promoting equality but feel that the value of humility is one that can be applied to social work as a whole:

> The field of inequality is a constantly changing one, with new challenges arising all the time. What is needed, then, is a degree of humility, a recognition that, however skilled, experienced or well informed we are, there is always a margin for error, and always scope for learning. (Thompson, 2003a, p. 236)

Humility, like any other skill, is something that can be developed over time.

Resilience

Social work is a demanding occupation that can be physically, mentally and emotionally draining. Sometimes we can feel weighed down by the pressures of the work and may want to give up. As argued earlier, the skills of stress management are important ones to develop. However, one aspect of this is the ability to be resilient to the pressures, demands, frustrations and disappointments of the work. These include:

- having to say 'no' to people when demand exceeds supply;
- encountering situations for which there is no apparent solution, even though it may be a very difficult and painful situation for the people concerned;
- applying for funding or resources on someone's behalf but being turned down;
- making good progress in a particular situation, but then having to abandon it because the person concerned withdraws his or her cooperation;
- team colleagues or others within a multidisciplinary network blocking progress by acting unprofessionally or by not doing what they agreed to do;

- receiving an unfair 'bad press' as a result of prejudices and stereotypes about 'bloody social workers';
- organizational changes or other management/local political initia-
  tives that complicate or exacerbate existing problems or pressures.

My argument is not that social workers should put up with all
the problems and pressures that come their way. However, many of the
problems are unavoidable or, although capable of resolution, may take
a long time to be resolved – leaving us with the challenge of having to
cope with them in the meantime. There is therefore a need to develop a
resilience to these factors that can undermine, obstruct or derail our
motivation, efforts or achievements. This is more than a dogged deter-
mination and can be seen to involve:

- a commitment to making a success of social work as far as possible
  (something closely linked to the value base);
- a willingness and ability to stand back from the situation and not let
  it get us down;
- a well-developed set of coping skills;
- a support network to be drawn upon as and when required.

A sense of humour can also be a very valuable resource to be able to
draw upon!

Partnership skills

Working in partnership has to be recognized as a highly skilled activity. It requires of us the ability to communicate and engage, to assess
and plan, to be sensitive and observant, and so on. It is therefore,
in many ways, an amalgam of so many other skills. For example, it
requires a degree of humility to accept that the professionals do not
have all the answers and clients have a major contribution to make to
resolving the difficulties that have been identified. However, there is
also the basic skill of working in partnership itself – being able and
willing to use power to empower.

In our interpersonal interactions, power is everpresent, in the
sense that people seek to influence each other and, in so doing, either
reflect or challenge existing power relations. Working in partnership
involves facilitating the collective use of power on the part of those
involved to meet needs, resolve difficulties and so on. An obstacle to
such partnership is the inappropriate use, by the worker, of his or her

power to coerce or exploit others. That is, if our efforts are geared towards pressurizing others into doing what we want them to do, partnership becomes more difficult, if not impossible, to achieve.

This is not to say that it is never necessary to use statutory powers to achieve particular ends, but this should be the exception, rather than the rule, as discussed in Chapter 1 – social work involves control as well as care. It is important not to slip into a medical model of social work, where the social worker is seen as the 'expert' who 'diagnoses' the problem and 'prescribes' a 'cure'. As we noted earlier, such a model has a tendency to disempower people and can therefore prove counterproductive. Avoiding the temptation to apply a medical model, particularly where others involved in the situation encourage you to adopt such an approach, is a skilled undertaking, requiring a great deal of presence of mind and an ability to resist unhelpful pressures.

Survival skills

'Survival skills' may sound a somewhat dramatic term, but they are none the less important skills to develop. I would divide them up into two groups:

1. *Self-care skills* This includes the self-management and time management skills mentioned above, but would also encompass the ability to recognize the satisfactions social work offers (avoiding the temptation to adopt a cynical and defeatist attitude that can lead to burnout), acknowledging the successes and achievements – however modest they may be – and maintaining the enthusiasm and commitment that are necessary for high-quality professional practice.
2. *Influencing skills* Success in social work depends to a large extent on others. The ability to influence individuals, groups and organizations is therefore a central part of the successful social worker's repertoire. Having little or no influence can leave the social worker frustrated, ineffectual and en route perhaps to major problems in the future. The ability to influence without coercing or exploiting is therefore an important one to develop.

It is important to emphasize that, by 'survival skills', I do not mean being defensive or 'covering one's back'. As the history of child protection has shown, there are many cases on record of workers who have focused on protecting themselves, rather than on the safety and well-being of the child, with the ironic result that the child suffers unnecessarily, therefore attracting criticism to the social worker and his or her handling of the situation. Defensive practice is not something to be encouraged. Focusing on good practice is a much more realistic strategy for survival in the demanding world of social work.

How do we develop skills?

It is fair comment to say that skill development comes with experience. However, it would be both naïve and inaccurate to assume that skills will necessarily develop spontaneously over a period of time. Experience provides the 'raw materials' for skill development, but this material has to be 'processed' if we are to maximize skill development and capitalize on the potential for learning that social work practice offers. Consequently, if we are to promote skill development to the best effect, we need to:

- *Reflect on practice*   See the discussion in Chapter 1 of reflective practice. Skill development is aided by understanding.
- *Be prepared to change*   If we are too conservative in our approach, too reluctant to do things differently, we will obstruct our own skill development.
- *Have faith in yourself*   Confidence in your own ability is an excellent spur to learning. If you do not have confidence in yourself, how can you expect others to have confidence in you?
- *Learn from others*   Simply copying from others can be a recipe for disaster, but there is still much we can learn from watching colleagues in action where possible.
- *Use supervision and training*   Opportunities to discuss your skills, and perhaps to try them out on training courses can be invaluable.
- *Don't get complacent*   Learning a new skill brings a degree of tension, but once that tension dissipates as we begin to become proficient, we can often relax and become complacent, failing to take the opportunity to continue to develop the skill concerned.

Conclusion

I hope that this chapter will not have proved too daunting in highlighting just how many skills are involved in social work and how important a role they play in achieving good practice. There are, though, two reassuring points worth emphasizing:

1. You already have a lot of the skills discussed here. We tend to develop them as part of growing up in modern society. Our task, then, for many of the skills concerned, is to build on our existing strengths, rather than to 'start from scratch'.
2. You are not expected to display a high level of skill right from the start. It is recognized that people need time and support to develop a comprehensive skills base. A major feature of professional training in social work is an emphasis on the development of skills, for example, through supervised practice on placement.

It is important to note that skill development is not only a challenge, in the sense of a problem to be solved, but also a source of considerable enjoyment and satisfaction. It is a very good platform for working together with colleagues to support each other in your professional development. And, finally, another positive point to note, is that many of the skills developed through reflective social work practice are also very useful in our private lives outside of a work context – they are a source of personal enrichment in their own right.

Guide to further learning

The CCETSW competences are detailed in CCETSW's own literature (CCETSW, 1996). In terms of skills development more broadly, Thompson (2002a) covers many of the skills discussed in this chapter.

As far as specific skills are concerned, the following are worth consulting: assessment: Milner and O'Byrne (2002); communication: Thompson (2003b); written work: Hopkins (1999a) and (1999b); self-awareness: Johnson (1993); self-management: Murdoch and Scutt (1993); presentation skills: Squirrell (1998); creativity: de Bono (1983); and partnership: Barker (1994) and Harrison et al. (2003).

Exercise 4

Consider the 15 sets of skills outlined in this chapter. For each of these, think about your own level of skill development. How confident do you feel about each of these areas? In what ways do you feel you need to develop? In particular can you 'prioritize' these by identifying what you see as the three most important? Use the space below to make some notes.

[Please note: there are no 'right answers' to this exercise. It is simply an opportunity for you to reflect on your skills and begin to consider ways of developing them.]

5

The value base

Introduction

Social work involves working with some of the most disadvantaged sections of the community and with people who, for a variety of reasons, are experiencing major problems and distress, often with unmet needs and other difficulties that may at times seem intractable. In view of this, it should be clear that social workers must guard strenuously against the possibility of exploiting or oppressing their clientele through unethical practices. Consequently, the question of moral values in social work has to be recognized as a major one, in terms of both its complexity and its ramifications. This chapter therefore examines the significance of values as a central feature of social work theory, policy and practice.

I shall begin by considering the basic question of 'What are values?', and then move on to explore the traditional values of social work and the more modern values associated with emancipatory practice.

What are values?

Banks (1995) points out the complexity associated with the term 'values':

> 'Values' is one of those words that tends to be used rather vaguely and has a number of different meanings. In everyday usage, 'values' is often used to refer to one or all of religious, moral, political or ideological principles, beliefs or attitudes. In the context of social work, however, it seems frequently to be used to mean: a set of fundamental moral/ethical principles to which social workers are/should be committed. (p. 4)

At its simplest, a value is something we hold dear, something we see as important and worthy of safeguarding. Consequently, values are an important influence on our actions and attitudes – they will encourage us to do certain things and to avoid certain others. In this way, values are not simply abstract concepts – they are very concrete in the sense that they have a very strong influence over what happens. They are a very strong force in shaping people's behaviour and responses to situations. It would therefore be very foolish to underestimate the significance of values in social work.

An important point to note is that values will continue to influence our actions even if we are not aware that they are doing so. That is, we do not have to be fully aware of what our values are, as they will have a bearing on the decisions we make and the steps that we take regardless of our degree of open awareness of them. For example, a worker may not be explicitly aware that he or she subscribes to a particular value (the importance of human dignity, for example) but none the less act fully in accordance with this (implicitly held) value. However, it can be argued that the more conscious we are of our own values, the more we are able to ensure that our actions are consistent with them.

At the other extreme, it is also possible for people to profess allegiance to a particular value but not actually put it into practice. These are known as 'espoused values': This involves expressing a commitment to one or more values (gender equality, for example) but not actually acting in accordance with this. As Preston-Shoot (1996) so aptly comments: 'values are only as good as the actions they prompt' (p. 31). A tokenistic approach to values in which people simply 'go through the motions' without actually embracing the values in and through their actions can be seen as not only dishonest but also potentially very harmful.

Before looking more closely at particular social work values, it is important to stress that the whole topic of values is an extremely complex one, and so it is unrealistic to expect (either now or at any stage in the future) to be able to establish a simple set of rules or procedures to follow in order to ensure ethical practice. The thorny issue of values is one that we are going to have to continue to wrestle with. Shardlow (2002a) captures the point well in the following passage:

> Getting to grips with social work values and ethics is rather like picking up a live, large and very wet fish from a running stream. Even if you are lucky enough to grab a fish, the chances are that just when you think you have caught it, the fish will vigorously slither out of your hands and

jump back in the stream. Values and ethics similarly slither through our fingers for a variety of reasons: we don't try hard to enough to catch them, preferring the practical business of doing social work; the subject matter, if we really investigate it, may sometimes seem complex, hard to grapple with and possibly obscure; there is a lack of conceptual clarity about many of the terms used that form part of the lexicon of 'social work values and ethics'; the boundaries of 'social work values and ethics' are imprecise and ill-defined, so the notion of what should constitute 'social work values and ethics' is itself part of a discussion about the nature of social work values. No doubt there are other reasons for not picking up this particular fish! (p. 30)

Traditional values

It has long been recognized that values have an important part to play in shaping social work policy and practice. Much has therefore been written about the value base of social work over a long period of time. Consequently, we can identify a set of traditional values that have been made explicit as a basis for practice. In particular, the work of Biestek (1961) has been especially influential. I shall therefore use his seven-point schema to begin to outline the basics of traditional social work values.

Individualization

This refers to the need to recognize each person as a unique individual in his or her own right. In a fast-moving and overcrowded modern world of mass production and consumption, we can readily recognize a wide range of situations in which people appear to lose their identity and are just treated as members of a crowd, rather than unique individuals in their own right. This social work value relates to the importance of making sure that clients and carers are not treated in this 'blanket' way, but rather are recognized for what they are: particular individuals with problems, concerns and needs which are specific to them and their circumstances.

Biestek explains individualization in the following terms:

Individualization is the recognition and understanding of each client's unique qualities and the differential use of principles and methods in assisting each towards a better adjustment. Individualization is based upon the right of human beings to be individuals and to be treated not just as *a* human being but as *this* human being with his personal differences. (1961, p. 25)

The fact that he uses the term 'adjustment' and refers to the client as 'he' indicates to us that Biestek is firmly rooted within a 'traditional' model of social work. We shall see below how this differs from a more modern perspective.

Individualization has important implications for practice. Although there may be many things in common with other situations, the particular combination of factors, what this means to the person concerned and how it is experienced, will be unique to each individual client at any given time. Failing to recognize this is to treat clients as representatives of broader categories, rather than as persons in their own right. In effect, this amounts to 'dehumanizing' clients, treating them as if they were things, rather than as important human beings with dignity and rights.

An example of where individualization is not respected would be a situation where a worker receiving a new referral does not undertake an assessment, but simply relies on stereotypes and assumptions: 'I know what to expect – I've dealt with this sort of situation before.' I encountered a further example of a neglect of this value at a planning meeting relating to an autistic child. A team manager present at the meeting stated that the boy's needs were those of 'an autistic child' and resisted attempts to explore the specific, individualized needs of that particular autistic boy.

Purposeful expression of feelings

The feelings dimension is an important part of social work. If people's feelings are not given due consideration, then it is unlikely that significant progress will be made (see Chapter 7). Giving clients the opportunity to vent and discuss their feelings is therefore an important part of good practice. This recognition reflects the psychodynamic roots of traditional social work, with its emphasis on inner psychological factors.

As a value principle, the purposeful expression of feelings relates to the recognition that clients should be enabled to talk about their feelings openly and not have to keep them submerged or repressed. To deny clients the opportunity to do this at a time of distress could be seen as adding insult to injury and is therefore regarded as unethical.

Biestek captures the point well when he argues that:

> Purposeful expression of feelings is recognition of the client's need to express his feelings freely, especially his negative feelings. The caseworker listens purposefully, neither discouraging nor condemning the expression of these feelings, sometimes even actually stimulating and encouraging them when they are therapeutically useful as part of the casework service. (1961, p. 35)

It is important to note, however, that Biestek is not simply advocating allowing or encouraging people to express their feelings in an unfettered way, as if this will somehow automatically lead to an improvement in the situation. Dealing with feelings is a skilful business (see Thompson, 2002a, Chapter 15), and so we should not underestimate the potential difficulties of adopting this value of purposeful expression of feelings.

Controlled emotional involvement

This principle follows on directly from the previous one in so far as it too relates to the emotional dimension of social work. Facilitating the purposeful expression of feelings is clearly important, but this must also be accompanied by an ability and willingness to respond sensitively and appropriately to the feelings being expressed. Just as the suppression of feelings by the worker can be seen as unethical, so too can the insensitive handling of feelings be seen as morally unacceptable.

Controlled emotional involvement entails:

- Recognizing that feelings play a very important role in social work – if we do not hold any real conviction about the significance of the feelings dimension, then we are unlikely to have sufficient sensitivity to it.
- Being able to 'tune in' to the feelings being expressed by the client (directly or indirectly), and appreciating what they mean to the individual concerned.
- Responding sensitively to these feelings by acknowledging them in a supportive way, using our communication skills to good effect.
- Being aware of our own feelings but not allowing these to stand in the way of responding appropriately – that is, neither ignoring our own feelings nor allowing ourselves to become emotionally 'involved'.

It should be clear, then, that the emotional element in social work is not only a challenge to our skills (in terms of how we deal with some very complex and demanding situations) but also a major ethical issue. Handling feelings appropriately is both a practice skill and a fundamental social work value.

Acceptance

Biestek acknowledges that this is a rather vague term and is difficult to pin down precisely. He tries to represent its meaning in the following passage:

> Acceptance is a principle of action wherein the caseworker perceives and deals with the client as he really is, including his strengths and weaknesses, his congenial and uncongenial qualities, his positive and negative feelings, his constructive and destructive attitudes and beha- viour, maintaining all the while a sense of the client's innate dignity and personal worth. (1961, p. 72)

As we shall see below, this has much in common with the notion of 'unconditional positive regard'. It refers to being prepared to work with someone whether or not we like them, whether or not we approve of them or what they may have done. The underlying ethical principle is that everyone is entitled to be treated with dignity and respect. This reflects the humanistic principle that every human being has value and, as Biestek puts it: 'No individual characteristic forfeits this value' (p. 73). That is, human dignity is recognized as something that everyone has as a right, rather than something that has to be earned or achieved by a particular individual.

This can sometimes be a difficult value to put into practice in cer- tain circumstances, particularly where someone has acted in such a way as to offend our other values. None the less, it remains the case that *acceptance* is a fundamental social work value, despite these difficulties.

Accepting someone as they are involves recognizing their strengths as well as weaknesses. Consequently, one important implication of this principle is that clients can and should be helped to draw on their own abilities and strengths. The social work task, in this regard, is to help the client realize his or her potential for self-help.

Non-judgemental attitude

Closely related to the value of acceptance is that of the need to adopt a non-judgemental attitude. It is not the social worker's role to *judge* individuals or families, in the sense of approving or disapproving of them. It is not a matter of 'assigning guilt or innocence, or client responsibility for the problems or needs' (Biestek, 1961, p. 90). That is, it is deemed unhelpful for workers to stand in judgement of their clients.

This is not to say that clients can do no wrong, or that the worker must approve of everything they do. While we may find a particular action unacceptable and therefore disapprove of it, we should not 'disapprove' of the person. This means that help should be offered in accordance with need and identified priorities, and not according to whether the individual client 'deserves' such help. For example, to deny someone a service because they have somehow contributed to their own problems (through excessive drinking, perhaps) is to run the risk of increasing pressures on that person, thus increasing the likelihood of their experiencing problems – perhaps creating a vicious circle in which a withholding of help leads to a worsening of the situation which, in turn, may lead to further judgements being made.

It is also important to note that a non-judgemental attitude is important as a basis for a sound working relationship. This is because such a relationship must be based on a degree of trust and respect – two things that are unlikely to be present if the worker indulges in being judgemental.

One common misunderstanding in relation to the value of being non-judgemental is a confusion between being judgemental and making professional judgements. The former is something to be avoided, for the reasons outlined here, while the latter is something that is a necessary part of good practice. The confusion arises from equating making a professional *judgement* (for example, in forming a picture of the situation as part of the process of undertaking an assessment) with being *judgemental* (in the sense of making a moral judgement by assigning guilt). The similarity in the terminology should not mislead us into thinking that the exercise of 'judgement' (that is, forming a professional opinion based on evidence and analysis) as part of day-to-day practice is necessarily unethical.

Client self-determination

This refers to the very important idea that social workers should play an active part in helping clients to help themselves, to make their own decisions and to take responsibility for their actions. Although the social work role can, and often does, involve the use of power and authority, it is generally recognized that the client should make the decisions and take the necessary steps to improve the situation wherever possible.

The social worker can play an important role in this by:

- Not trying to 'play God' by overplaying the power and influence they have at their disposal.
- Helping clients to recognize the choices they can or must make.
- Helping clients to explore the options available to them and the likely consequences.
- Boosting confidence where possible and appropriate.
- Exploring and, where possible, removing or undermining cultural and structural barriers to self-determination.
- Increasing, where possible, the range of options available, for example through the provision of resources and/or the use of advocacy and networking.
- Providing, or facilitating access to, the information needed to make an informed decision.
- Resisting the temptation to allow a dependency relationship to develop, for example by encouraging clients to make their own decisions and supporting them in doing so.

It should be noted, however, that there are two common misconceptions as far as client self-determination is concerned, and it is therefore important that we should guard against these:

1. To promote the value of self-determination is *not* to deny that the social worker should never seek to limit or constrain the client's actions or choices. It remains the case that some actions are likely to be unacceptable (violence or abuse, for example) and will therefore need to be curbed. The exercise of the worker's authority in such cases is not a denial of client self-determination, but rather a limit to it. Biestek himself acknowledged that there had to be limits to self-determination as a result of broader moral and/or legal considerations. Client self-determination is therefore not to be equated with licence or an abandonment of legal or agency responsibilities. It would be naïve in the extreme to regard client self-determination as absolute or boundless.
2. Social factors such as poverty, deprivation, racism and so on do not rob the individuals concerned of their ability to exercise self-determination. It is a mistake to assume that social factors,

although clearly quite significant in limiting the life chances of certain groups and individuals, have the effect of denying such people the opportunity to make choices and decisions for themselves. It is certainly the case that poverty and other such social problems reduce the actual options for action, but, of course, to reduce available options is not to take away the ability to choose altogether. Clearly, someone living in poverty has fewer options than a wealthy person, but none the less retains the capacity to make his or her own decisions within the constraints of his or her present circumstances.

Confidentiality

To enable a client to feel comfortable enough to discuss sensitive, personal matters, it is important that they feel that they are able to speak openly without the information they provide being made widely available. That is, confidentiality is necessary as a basis for social work interventions based on trust and honesty. Biestek expresses the idea in the following terms:

> Confidentiality is the preservation of secret information concerning the client which is disclosed in the professional relationship. Confidentiality is based on a basic right of the client; it is an ethical obligation of the caseworker and is necessary for effective casework service. The client's right, however, is not absolute. Moreover, the client's secret is often shared with other professional persons within the agency and in other agencies; the obligation then binds all equally. (1961, p. 121)

There are two important issues arising from this passage:

1. Confidentiality is not absolute. That is, there are limits to the operation of confidentiality. For example, where information comes to light which has a bearing on the safety of another person, it may be necessary to disclose that information for the sake of the protection of the individual even if this involves breaching confidentiality. This is especially the case in relation to child abuse where there is a clearly recognized duty to share information that will contribute to the child's safety, despite confidentiality.
2. Confidentiality is to the agency, rather than to the individual worker. That is, social workers need to make it clear that information given may have to be recorded and may therefore be

available to other staff within the organization (the team manager, for example) or may even be shared with staff from other agencies as part of multidisciplinary collaboration. The boundaries of confidentiality are therefore complex and need to be considered carefully.

These seven ethical principles have proven to be very influential in social work and continue to underpin much of contemporary practice. However, they are not, of course, the only values to have a bearing on practice. In particular, one which does not feature in Biestek's work but which is compatible with it is that of 'respect for persons'.

Respect for persons

Shardlow (2002a, p. 35) explains the notion of respect for persons in the following terms:

> This moral notion was fully explored by Downie and Telfer (1969). As a moral principle, 'respect for persons' is derived from Kant's moral principle of the *categorical imperative*. This is variously written, but amongst the best-known formulations are:
>
> > I ought never to act except in such a way that I can also will that my maxim should become a universal law. (Kant, 1785, in Paton, 1948: 67)
> >
> > Act in such a way that you always treat humanity whether in your own person or in the person of any other, never simply as a means but always at the same time as an end. (Kant,1785, in Paton, 1948: 91)

To act in accordance with this value, therefore, is to treat other people in such a way as you feel all people should treat each other. For example, you should not lie to a client unless you feel it is acceptable for all social workers to lie to clients. Similarly, you should not seek to manipulate people by using them simply as a means to an end.

Although Kant's moral philosophy is quite complex and difficult to grasp, the basic point is quite a simple one really, namely the importance of treating people with respect – not treating them in a way that you would object to if other people treated you like that.

In terms of traditional values, the work of Carl Rogers (1961) has also been influential. His 'person-centred' approach to counselling has helped to shape social work values. In particular, three key concepts have played a significant part in developing our thinking on these issues and guiding our actions. These are each briefly explained below.

Congruence

This refers to the practitioner's willingness and ability to be genuine and open, not playing games or being manipulative. As Rogers (1961) comments:

> It has been found that personal change is facilitated when the psychotherapist is what he *is*, when in the relationship with his client he is genuine and without 'front' or facade, openly being the feelings and attitudes which at that moment are flowing *in* him. We have coined the term 'congruence' to try to describe this condition. (p. 61)

If a positive working relationship based on trust and respect is to develop, then a degree of such 'congruence' or genuineness must be achieved. To attempt to influence others without this could be seen as highly unethical.

An example of congruence in action would be where a social worker talks openly about feelings, in a genuine attempt to move the situation forward, rather than trying to cover them up or distort them. Clearly, this value has much in common with the existentialist concept of authenticity and the rejection of bad faith.

Empathy

This is similar to, but also different from, the better-known idea of 'sympathy'. To 'have sympathy' for someone means to have the same feelings as they do. For example, to sympathize with someone who is feeling very sad is to share some of that sadness ourselves. Empathy, by contrast, involves recognizing, and responding to, the other person's feelings without necessarily having those feelings.

This is a very skilful activity, as it involves having a degree of control over our own feelings while remaining open and sensitive to the other person's feelings. If we do not manage to achieve the former (a degree of control over our own feelings), then we run the risk of becoming emotionally involved at too deep a level, and also of exhausting ourselves through emotional overload. If we were to take on board and share the feelings of all the people we work with, we would very quickly reach a point where we could not function – where we would be so burdened down with emotions of various kinds that we would be unable to deal with our day-to-day tasks, let alone anything more demanding.

Achieving empathy is therefore not only a social work value, in the sense of an important ethical principle to aspire to, but also a practical necessity to avoid creating a situation where we cannot cope with the intense emotional pressures.

Unconditional positive regard

This refers to the need to work positively and constructively with *all* clients, and not just those that we approve of or feel comfortable with. That is, our positive regard should be unconditional – something that all clients are entitled to. This combines elements of two of Biestek's values, namely acceptance and a non-judgemental attitude.

If we do not live up to this value, there is a very real danger that we shall discriminate against certain sections of the community, giving some people a lower standard of service because there is something about them that we are not happy with. This can be seen as a significant abuse of professional power and is therefore understandably seen as ethically unacceptable. It means that clients are given a quality of service, according not to their needs, but to the whim of the worker.

A good example of where unconditional positive regard can and should apply is in work with sex offenders. If, in dealing with a man who has sexually abused children, we allow our feelings of disapproval or even revulsion to manifest themselves as a negative or unhelpful attitude towards him, then we are far less likely to be able to influence him positively and help him move away from sexually abusive behaviour. This means that, unless we are able to demonstrate unconditional positive regard in examples such as this, then we are reducing our chances of effective intervention with him and thus indirectly contributing to the continuance of his offending behaviour. That is, we would be allowing our negative feelings towards someone to prevent us from working effectively with him.

Clearly, the development of unconditional positive regard is a difficult and challenging task and can sometimes mean that we have to deal with our own strong feelings. This is where high-quality supervision can be a major asset in helping us to deal with our own feelings and to enable us to work positively in such circumstances (see Morrison, 2000).

It is interesting to note, that, in the following passage, Jordan (1979) reflects very clearly a strong Rogerian value base, combining elements of all three of the values into one statement:

> In suggesting that to be helpful the helper must be a real person, I am making it clear I think helping is not simply a skill or expertise or

technique. Helping is a test of the helper as a person. It involves the disciplined use of the whole of the personality. This includes the helper's own 'bad' feelings – his [sic] sadness, anger, fear, greed and cowardice. He has to be in touch with these things in himself in order to be truly open to the other person's distress. Yet he has also to retain his own values and standards, his own strengths and virtues. He has to recognise that the other person's feelings and fantasies are real to him, and to share in the discomfort of them, yet also to stay in touch with his own reality. (p. 26)

The values that have derived from Rogers' work are clearly not entirely separate from the work of Biestek and others. Indeed, they are very compatible and there is certainly scope for further exploration of the linkages and overlaps across the field of traditional values.

It should be clear from this brief overview of some of the traditional values underpinning social work that a major emphasis is on the value and dignity of the individual. Indeed, Plant (1970) argues that the concept of 'respect for persons' encapsulates many of the values associated with social work. It is important, then, to stress that social work is traditionally a person-centred undertaking, with a focus on supporting the unique individual in dealing with personal and social challenges that arise in the course of our lives.

Emancipatory values

In the 1960s social work came under attack for adopting too narrow and individualistic a focus, failing to take adequate account of the broader social and political context of social work practice. This led to the development of what became known as 'radical social work', which in turn laid the foundations for anti-discriminatory practice (Thompson, 2001). The changes in theory and practice associated with this development of awareness of wider social factors have been accompanied by developments in the value base, with the emergence of new values that go beyond the individualism of traditional social work and emphasize the importance of power, inequality, social justice and so on.

The more sociologically explicit focus of contemporary social work is sometimes misinterpreted as a replacement for the psychological insights of earlier forms of theory and practice, rather than as a transcendence of them. It is therefore important to emphasize that the more up-to-date values presented here are intended as a supplement and bolster to the traditional values already discussed, rather than as a replacement for them. My argument, then, is not that the traditional values were in some respect 'wrong', but rather that they did not go far enough – they were too narrow and individualistic in their focus. The aim is not to ignore the individual but to see him or her in the broader context of the range of cultural and structural factors which have such a strong bearing on social work interventions.

I shall present a number of values which are more consistent with this broader perspective but, as with the traditional values outlined above, it should be recognized that I am not claiming that this list is complete or by any means exhaustive. The subject of values is an enormous one, and there is certainly not enough space in one book, let alone one chapter, to do justice to the subject. What follows is therefore necessarily selective.

De-individualization

While it is certainly the case that it is important to recognize the uniqueness of the individual, it can also be argued that we should recognize in addition that we are not *just* unique individuals. That is, there are significant patterns that can be recognized (significant social formations, for example) which also play an important role in shaping our circumstances, our needs, problems and potential solutions.

Thompson *et al.* (1994b) argue that 'de-individualization' is needed in addition to individualization so that we are not discouraged from seeing clients in their wider context, particularly within the context of membership of oppressed groups:

> For example, in dealing with a woman with depression, the significance of gender can be highlighted (Brown and Harris, 1978) and aspects of depression can be related to expectations of female roles in society. In this way, the classic mistake of encouraging women to be more 'feminine' can be avoided. They can be helped to understand their feelings in the context of finding a positive thread of meaning rather than simply slotting into an accepted social role – especially when it may very well be that such oppressive gender expectations played a significant part in the onset of the depression, for example in terms of domestic violence, restricted opportunities for personal fulfilment, or sexual abuse. (p. 18)

The values of individualization and de-individualization are therefore not in opposition. Rather, it is a question of seeing individuals as *both* unique in their own right *and* part of a broader web of social and political factors.

Equality

A common mistake is to assume that equality is the same as uniformity, that the best way to ensure equality is to treat everybody the same. Of course, the problem with this point of view is that it fails to recognize that 'treating everybody the same' simply has the effect of reinforcing existing inequalities. That is, someone who is disadvantaged in some way will continue to be disadvantaged (and may have their disadvantage increased) when being treated in exactly the same way as someone who has far more life chances, much greater access to resources and considerably more power to draw upon. To promote equality, therefore, is a complex matter and cannot simply be reduced to treating everybody the same. It is more a case of treating everyone with equal fairness, rather than treating everybody the same, as treating someone fairly often means treating them differently from other people (because their needs are different from other people's).

The existence of large-scale inequalities in terms of class, race/ ethnicity, gender, age, disability, sexual identity and so on is an important fact to recognize but it is only comparatively recently that social work has placed equality in a prominent place on its agenda. Such inequalities are particularly relevant to social work, as so many social work clients experience one or more of these forms of disadvantage as a major feature of their lives. A willingness to acknowledge – and a preparedness to tackle – such inequalities has therefore now come to be recognized as a key value of social work.

While traditional social work values would no doubt have rejected prejudice and discrimination as unethical practices, the individualist emphasis of such values would not have enabled us to recognize that discrimination operates not only at the level of personal prejudice, but also in terms of shared norms, values, assumptions, meanings and stereotypes as well as the structural level of power relations, social institutions and so on (Thompson, 2001). Promoting equality is therefore far more complex than avoiding personal prejudice or bigotry. The roots of inequality run far more deeply than that.

Social justice

Social work to a large extent involves working predominantly with those sectors of society which have a higher than average share of poverty, deprivation and social disadvantage. Many social work clients have been victims of abuse, exploitation or degradation at the hands of more powerful groups or individuals. Most are subject, as I mentioned above, to one or more forms of inequality or social disadvantage. Social injustice is therefore something that social workers encounter on more or less a daily basis.

In view of this, it should not be surprising to note that social justice is now increasingly being seen as an important social work value. To work alongside such injustice without seeking to address it as a serious social problem can clearly be seen as an unethical form of practice, in so far as it involves leaving oppressive structures and established practices intact. It has been argued (Skidmore *et al.,* 1997) that the very heart of social work is: 'to dignify the human process'. Ignoring or colluding with social injustice is clearly not compatible with any such attempt to dignify the human process.

Partnership

At its simplest level, partnership means working *with* clients, rather than doing things *to* or *for* them. It involves moving away from the outmoded view of social work as a form of 'social medicine' in which the expert social worker diagnoses the problem and prescribes a cure or 'treatment programme'. This medical model is gradually being replaced by a partnership-based approach in which:

- Assessment of the situation is carried out by the worker in close cooperation with the client(s) and, where appropriate, the carer(s) – with a view to establishing agreement on the nature of the problem, the identified needs, the objectives to aim for and possible plans of action for responding to them.
- Intervention involves the relevant parties working together to take the necessary steps to resolve or minimize problems, to meet needs and do whatever is needed to meet the agreed objectives.
- The situation is jointly reviewed at appropriate points and, ideally, jointly evaluated when the piece of work comes to an end.

This can also be taken a step further by involving clients in the planning of services, the development of policy and so on – what is often referred to as a participation or user-involvement approach.

However, partnership is not just about working with clients. It also involves collaborating with other professionals as part of a multi-disciplinary approach. That is, partnership involves recognizing that the best results are to be obtained by working as effectively as possible in tandem with colleagues from other agencies (health visitors, doctors, community psychiatric nurses, housing officers, teachers and so on). Collaboration with others is a skilled activity and can be quite challenging at times. However, the benefits of a united, concerted effort are generally well worth the effort (but see Chapter 7 for a discussion of some of the difficulties that can be encountered in this regard).

Citizenship

A major implication of the status of being a citizen is having certain rights – and this is why citizenship is an important value, because it places emphasis on *rights* and *social inclusion*.

As far as rights are concerned, the Disabled People's Movement has pointed out that disabled people's rights are often neglected as a result of social workers' focus on providing care services rather than on supporting the right to be able to participate in society in much the same way as non-disabled people (Oliver and Sapey, 1999). This also relates closely to the notion of social inclusion – challenging the marginalization, stigmatization and social exclusion that so many social work clients experience. To be a citizen means having social rights and being included in mainstream social life. In this respect, much social work practice plays a pivotal role promoting or undermining the citizenship status of particular individuals, families or groups who are otherwise prone to social exclusion.

Lister (1997) has updated the traditional notion of citizenship to make it compatible with emancipatory values. She does this by reviewing the idea of being a 'citizen' and highlighting the need to incorporate a broader gender perspective. That is, she points out how the traditional notion of citizenship is a male-oriented one, paying little attention to women's needs or contribution. Similarly, Taylor (1996a) argues that traditional notions of citizenship tend to be eurocentric in their focus and need to take on board a broader understanding of its international context and the significance of race and ethnicity.

Citizenship can therefore be seen as a two-edged sword. In some respects it represents a form of elitism, a means of excluding certain groups from participation in mainstream social life. However, it can also be used as an emancipatory value by focusing on social inclusion and rights. As Taylor (1996a) comments:

> The concept of citizenship has a radical purchase in opposing the authoritarian denial of civil rights and liberties. In the context of a

restructuring of welfare its appeal is clear: a reassertion of claims against the state and as a demand for just and equal treatment and demands for equal rights. (p. 165)

Empowerment

This is a widely used term but also one that is contested and subject to varying definitions and usages (Gomm, 1993). At its simplest level, it refers to the process of gaining greater control over one's life and circumstances. However, its use in social work extends beyond that, to take account of the discrimination and oppression experienced by clients. That is, empowerment is more than the traditional notion of 'enabling'. It is geared towards helping to equip people for the challenges of tackling the social disadvantages and inequalities they face. Empowerment is not only a psychological process but also a social and political one.

Solomon (1976) provides a helpful definition when she writes of empowerment as a:

> process whereby persons who belong to a stigmatized social category throughout their lives can be assisted to develop and increase skills in the exercise of interpersonal influence and the performance of valued social roles. (p. 12, cited in Dalrymple and Burke, 1995, p. 50)

A common misunderstanding is that empowerment involves the social worker 'giving away' his or her power. This is based on an oversimplified view of power in which it is seen as something that can be given from one person to another in a simple or straightforward way:

> It is commonly assumed by many that empowerment involves taking away the worker's power. However, if this is done, it will of course make him or her less effective and therefore of less value or use. Empowerment is a matter of helping people gain greater control over their lives, helping them to become better equipped to deal with the problems and challenges they face – especially those that involve seeking to counter or overcome discrimination and oppression. (Thompson, 1998a, p. 9)

Power is an extremely complex concept (see Thompson, 2003a, Chapter 2) which operates at different levels. The process of empowerment is therefore also complex and operates at several levels (see Humphries, 1996) and in different ways. Fook (2002) illustrates this point well when she argues that:

People do not fit easily into 'powerful' or 'powerless' groupings, some-times having membership of both at the same time. As well, members of powerless groups do not necessarily agree on the form of their em-powerment. Some people may experience the very same experience as empowering and others as disempowering. Sometimes what is em-powering for some might actually detract from the empowerment of others. (p. 47)

As an emancipatory value, empowerment is not simply a matter of 'enabling' or 'facilitating'. It also involves taking seriously the significance of the disadvantage and oppression that are so character-istic of so many clients' day-to-day experience. Helping people 'func-tion' better at an interpersonal level without connecting this with the broader sociopolitical context of their problems and circumstances is not what empowerment is about. Rather, it involves playing a part in connecting the personal to the political – for example, by helping a woman who has experienced violence at the hands of her partner to become aware of the broader social problem of domestic violence and its links with male power in society, so that she does not see her own situation as simply an unfortunate development or, worse still, something she has brought on herself (Mullender, 1996).

Authenticity

Authenticity is an existentialist concept, as discussed in Chapter 1. It refers to the recognition of 'radical freedom' – that is, the acknowl-edgement that each individual is not only free to choose but also *has* to choose, in the sense that we are responsible for our own actions. What happens to us is partly beyond our control, but also owes a great deal to the decisions we make, the steps we take and so on. And, of course, it should be remembered that to avoid making a decision (for example, by using delaying tactics or being unwilling to face up to a particular situation) is in itself a decision – a choice made by the individual concerned. Similarly, not taking a particular course of action can have just as many consequences as acting – what we choose not to do may be just as significant as what we do do, if not more so.

Authenticity therefore involves drawing out the implications of this responsibility without trying to deny or minimize the fact that each of us has it. To be authentic is to refuse to fall into the trap of seeing the causes of our behaviour as being beyond our control, to avoid using convenient excuses, such as: 'I can't help it, that's the way I am'. This is not to say that each of us is entirely responsible for what happens to us, but it does mean that we do play a part through our own choices and actions (or inactions). Authenticity involves being able to recognize the boundary between those aspects of our lives that we can control and those that we cannot, and making sure that what belongs in the first category does not get assigned to the second.

This is an important social work value at two levels. First, for social workers, it is vitally important that we recognize our own responsibilities and do not try to shirk from the part we play in the situations we encounter. That is, if we are not able to acknowledge the impact of our own choices and actions, then it is doubtful whether we are safe to be working in situations where we can have such an important bearing on the lives and well-being of people who are often very vulnerable as a result of the circumstances they are in. Second, if we are to play a part in empowering clients, then, we have to be able to assist them in achieving authenticity where necessary. For example, if we wish people to have greater control over their lives so that they are in a stronger position to tackle the disadvantages and inequalities they face, then they must surely first recognize the extent of their abilities to influence situations – that is, the degree of freedom and responsibility they have in relation to their own choices and actions. Empowerment is often a matter of helping people remove barriers to progress – and authenticity has a major part to play in this, as so often many of the barriers we face are partly self-made (for example, a person may lack confidence as a result of having internalized comments made by teachers and others that he or she was of low ability). Some forms of social work can be helpful in constructively confronting and undermining such barriers – helping people to help themselves.

I believe it is particularly important that social workers embrace the value of authenticity, as to fail to do so has major ethical consequences. Again, this is at two levels. First, how can I honestly expect clients to change and move on in their lives if I feel that I, as a worker, am not able to grow and develop, if I believe that 'I am what I am and I can't change'? Clearly it would be very dishonest of me to expect clients to undertake what I am not prepared to do myself. Second, if I deny client authenticity, then I too am contributing to the range of barriers that may well have held them back in their lives – I become part of the problem, rather than part of the solution. My negative and defeatist attitude ('They can't change and I don't suppose they ever will') could be very destructive. This is not to say that positive change is always possible or is an easy thing to achieve, but if we begin with the assumption that change is not possible, then we contribute to a 'self-fulfilling prophecy' – that is, our negative attitude makes the negative outcome all the more likely (see Chapter 6 for a discussion of the danger of defeatist practice).

Conclusion

Griseri (1998) makes the point that values are 'a combination of cognitive and emotive factors' (p. vii). They are not simply rational matters that we can resolve through logical argument. Nor are they purely emotional matters that cannot be subjected to rigorous scrutiny. They are an interesting combination of thoughts and feelings, and they are, of course, closely linked to actions. As in social life more broadly, thoughts, feelings and actions intertwine quite significantly and in quite complex and intricate ways. Where values are concerned, this 'intertwining' can be particularly complex.

Clearly, then, the question of values in social work is never going to be an easy one to address. It will remain a challenging subject and one that will no doubt exercise the minds of generations of social workers to come. We should not, however, be disheartened by this, but rather recognize it as one of the stimulating challenges of social work – one of those things that means that, whatever else it may be, social work as a professional practice is never boring, never without interest, stimulation or challenge.

I referred earlier to Shardlow's (2002a) point that values have a certain 'slippery' quality. No doubt this chapter has helped to confirm just how difficult values can be to grasp. However, it is to be hoped that, while not offering definitive answers (no book can realistically do that), this chapter has gone some way towards clarifying the role of values in social work and provided at least some foundation for building a better and more sophisticated understanding of these very important issues.

It should be clear from this chapter that values are one of those things that we will need to wrestle with for as long as we practise. Values arise from different people dealing with life's complexities and 'existential challenges' in different ways, from different perspectives, and with different objectives in mind. The values picture is therefore one that is constantly changing, a kaleidoscope of a wide range of issues, each with a bearing on the situations we encounter, and each with its own intricacies and nuances.

However, what is worth emphasizing is that this 'kaleidoscope effect' is not a problem to be solved, but rather a feature of the complex territory we, as professional social workers, occupy. Indeed, the word 'professional' is particularly apt, as I would see the need to wrestle with these complexities as a basic component of professionalism. If values were a simple matter that could be resolved by a rulebook or manual of procedures to be followed slavishly, we would not need to have professional practitioners schooled in the arts of dealing with complex, messy and changeable situations. We would simply need 'social technicians', rather than the flexible, reflective practitioners on which high-quality professional social work depends.

Guide to further learning

Banks (1995) provides a useful overview of values in social work, while Hugman and Smith (1995) provide an insightful set of readings on various aspects of ethical and value issues. Shardlow (2002a) is a good starting point, with Shardlow (2002b) exploring the issues in more depth.

Biestek (1961) now seems very dated but none the less has some worthwhile points to consider as a starting point at least. My own work has concentrated a great deal on emancipatory values and related issues, and so Thompson (1995a), Thompson (2001) and Thompson (2003a) are all relevant. Humphries (1996) provides a helpful outlook on empowerment, as do Braye and Preston-Shoot (1995). Fook (2002) is also very good on aspects of emancipatory values.

Lister (1997) is an interesting text dealing with citizenship from a feminist perspective. Barry and Hallett (1998) cover issues relating to discrimination under the heading of 'social exclusion'.

Partnership is covered in Harrison *et al.* (2003).

Exercise 5

The basis of this exercise is an opportunity for you to consider your own values. What are the principles you believe in? What values underpin your approach to people and their problems? You may find it helpful to discuss these issues with someone you know well and whose views you trust. Use the space below to make some notes.

6

Achieving good practice

Introduction

Social work is a very responsible professional activity which brings with it many pressures. It is understandable, then, that some practitioners have little ambition beyond surviving those pressures and simply getting through the day. However, 'understandable' and 'acceptable' are not the same thing. Such an approach falls far short of high-quality practice and is therefore unnecessarily self-limiting.

This chapter is therefore geared towards exploring what is involved in establishing high standards of practice. What is good practice? How do we achieve it? What steps do we need to take? These are some of the questions to be addressed. I shall explore what I regard as some of the essential components of good practice, explaining what they are and why I think they are so important. Inevitably, of course, this reflects *my* view of what constitutes good practice. While the ideas presented here are not particularly controversial, it none the less has to be recognized that the whole area is a contested one. Different people will have different perspectives on what good practice is.

The definition of 'good practice' is a major debate in its own right. This is partly because the notion of 'good practice' is linked to (1) our conception of what social work is and what it is for (as discussed in Chapter 1); and (2) our value base which, as we saw in Chapter 5, is not a simple or straightforward matter. It is therefore important that you think carefully about these issues and come to your own conclusions about this. This chapter acts in many ways as a summary of many of the important points made in earlier chapters about the nature of good practice.

Avoiding dangerous practice

It is widely accepted that the aim of social work is to 'do good' – that is, to respond to problems and unmet needs and make situations better for those involved. When we think in terms of success or failure, then, it is easy to phrase this in one simple question: has our intervention succeeded or failed in making this situation better? However, this misses out a very significant issue, in so far as it fails to recognize that social work intervention can actually make situations worse:

> It would be naïve in the extreme to fail to recognize that social work intervention is capable of not only making a positive difference to people's lives but also doing considerable harm. The social worker has a great deal of power, and such power can result in successful or unsuccessful outcomes. However, the absence of success can be much more than failure – intervention can also have an extremely detrimental effect on individuals, families and groups. This can include:
>
> - breaking up families
> - reducing self-esteem
> - creating dependency
> - reinforcing stigma, discrimination and oppression.
>
> Consequently, it is important to ensure, as far as possible, that intervention avoids inflicting such harm. The need to avoid dangerous practice is therefore of crucial concern for practitioners, managers and educators. (Thompson and Bates, 1998, p. 6)

The paper from which this quotation is taken goes on to describe five particular forms of dangerous practice. I shall follow the same pattern here in warning of the problems associated with practice that could be described as: routinized, defensive, defeatist, chaotic, or oppressive.

Routinized practice

It would, of course, be totally unworkable to try to tackle a heavy workload without relying on routines of some description. To attempt to deal with each aspect of work as a unique situation that needs to be carefully assessed before we can respond to it would quickly lead us to a situation where we were hopelessly overloaded with tasks, and no time or energy left over to complete them. It is clear, then, that routines do have a place in social work practice. They can be very useful for dealing with simple, repetitive tasks that require little or no concentration.

However, the problem comes when practitioners extend the use of routines to the point of where they apply them to situations that are far more complex and demanding than anything a routine response could realistically deal with. This is the point at which practice can get dangerous. The dangers include:

- alienating or offending the client by failing to take a serious interest in their problems and needs;
- missing or overlooking important aspects of the situation because untested assumptions have been relied upon;
- falling foul of stereotypes due to a failure to obtain sufficient information to form a more accurate and reliable picture;
- proposing inappropriate courses of action because the complexities of the situation have not been appreciated;
- missing opportunities for learning and professional development; and
- missing opportunities for job satisfaction, thereby increasing the chances of stress and burnout (see Chapter 7).

Routinized practice may result from work overload, from a lack of confidence on the part of the worker, from a team or organizational culture which encourages such practice, or indeed from any combination of these. Whatever its causes, however, it should be perfectly clear that good practice in social work must be non-routinized – that is, it must not extend the use of routines into aspects of practice where a more individualized and reflective approach is called for (see the discussion of Reflective practice below).

An important skill in this regard is the ability to distinguish between those situations where a routinized approach is safe and appropriate and those where it is far from appropriate – and therefore far from safe. It perhaps goes without saying that those aspects of practice that involve direct, face-to-face contact with people should certainly not be carried out on a routinized basis. While we may all develop our own preferred patterns of working, we need to be very careful to make sure that we do not allow these to become so comfortable that we use them in situations where they are potentially very dangerous.

Defensive practice

Social workers are often criticized in the media and elsewhere, whether such criticism is deserved or not. In addition, many social workers work in large, impersonal bureaucracies where it may not feel safe to do anything that could potentially go wrong. In view of this, it is not surprising that a defensive, 'cover your back' mentality has become a common pattern of thinking for many practitioners and managers. Unfortunately, this type of attitude can be extremely dangerous. This is because a defensive approach can lead to:

- tensions between worker and client – tensions which may be misinterpreted, for example as nervousness or a lack of confidence, thus undermining the development of a positive professional relationship;
- tensions between worker and colleagues in other agencies, possibly leading to a breakdown in effective multidisciplinary collaboration;
- important aspects of the situation being missed or misconstrued because the worker is concentrating too narrowly on potential risk factors;
- a reluctance to explore issues as fully as they merit in case such exploration leads to a situation the worker does not want to face;
- missed opportunities for learning and professional development due to too narrow a focus on the situation;
- missed opportunities for job satisfaction – defensive practice is not an enjoyable or rewarding form of practice.

The irony of defensive practice, of course, is that it actually *increases* the chances of a worker 'getting into trouble'. Where the social worker loses focus on the task in hand and replaces this with an emphasis on defensiveness, he or she makes it far more likely that something will go wrong and therefore that a complaint will be made or an investigation, inquiry or court case will reveal that the worker's approach was not a helpful one in so far as a focus on achieving the social work task was replaced by a focus on 'playing it safe'. Clearly, the best way for a worker to ensure that he or she stays out of trouble is to concentrate on *good* practice, rather than *defensive* practice. As Brechin *et al.* (2000) so aptly put it, we should be aiming for 'practice which is defensible rather than defensive' (p. xi).

Unfortunately, some organizations have a very pervasive culture of defensiveness. That is, the whole organization may be unwilling to take risks, putting a lot of pressure on its staff to avoid risky situations wherever possible – making it difficult, but not impossible, for committed social workers to engage in good (non-defensive) practice. It has to be recognized, though, that social work inevitably involves taking risks (Parton *et al.,* 1997; Kemshall and Pritchard, 1996), and so it is very short-sighted indeed for both individual staff and organizations to focus on risk avoidance at the expense of seeking to maximize effectiveness through good practice.

Defeatist practice

It has to be recognized that social work is *hard* work. It has its successes and rewards, but it also brings with it very many failures, frustrations and problems. It is easy to understand how, in certain circumstances, some practitioners can find it difficult to keep a balanced perspective and weigh up the positives against the negatives, resulting in a form of defeatism. This is illustrated in the following practice example:

> Lynn was a student on placement at a residential centre for people with alcohol-related problems. She began the placement with considerable enthusiasm but soon met a barrier. Whatever ideas she suggested, her practice teacher undermined and devalued them with her pessimistic and defeatist outlook. Lynn soon began to feel that nothing was going to be possible apart from containment and moral support. She was beginning to feel downhearted about the whole experience when another worker at the centre reassured her by commenting that he hoped her practice teacher's defeatist attitude was not going to rub off on her. (Thompson and Bates, 1998, p. 11)

Social work is not the sort of undertaking where successful outcomes are necessarily a daily experience, and so we have to be clear about what we mean by success and how often we should expect to be able to celebrate it. In particular, we should bear in mind that:

- many of the cases social workers deal with involve trying to prevent a deterioration or breakdown in the situation – maintaining the status quo is therefore often a success in its own right, even though it may not feel like it;
- circumstances are often such that factors beyond our control prevent us from making progress or achieving our agreed objectives – but we must recognize that, if we have done everything we could reasonably have been expected to, then this too is a form of success, albeit limited, as we have succeeded in maximizing the chances of positive outcomes; we have played our part to the best of our ability and can take some pride in that;

- significant successes are like gold nuggets – they make up for much of the time spent apparently getting nowhere.

Social work is not the type of occupation where success and job satisfaction are handed to you 'on a plate' – rather, it is the sort of work where success often runs alongside failure and where the occasional notable success keeps us going until the next breakthrough.

In view of this, it is important for practitioners and managers to recognize that things not working out, not always getting where we wanted to go, or situations falling apart on us are often par for the course. Social workers deal with what are often extremely complex and entrenched problems and have only limited resources available to deal with these. We therefore have to be realistic about how much can be achieved. However, being realistic and being defeatist are certainly not the same thing. The former can and should be a platform for good practice, while the latter is clearly a recipe for bad practice.

Chaotic practice

Parnell (1995) makes the point that, although time management skills can easily be appreciated as an important part of the social worker's repertoire of skills, they do not feature very much in the social work literature or as part of the curriculum of professional training. And yet to practise without being able to manage one's time and workload effectively is clearly quite problematic. A worker who is not able to achieve success in the following areas runs the very serious risk of practising dangerously:

- managing a diary – making sure that we are not double booked, and that we turn up in the right place at the right time;
- setting priorities to make sure that the most important things get done first;
- communicating effectively with people as and when required, not forgetting to keep people informed of what is going on;
- keeping records up to date;
- being realistic about what can and cannot be achieved in the timescale – an overloaded worker can be a very dangerous worker.

Skimping on these aspects of practice can be dangerous in a number of ways. For example, I have met many social workers who are very skilled communicators but they regularly fail to use their skills to good effect because their disorganized approach to work means that they often do not communicate when they should. And, of course, break-downs in communication are widely recognized as a major cause of problems within social work. Similarly, love them or hate them, records are an important part of social work practice and not an administrative chore to be avoided – failing to keep records up to date could have disastrous consequences if someone needed to intervene in that situation in your absence (while you were on leave, for example).

There are clearly problems associated with a chaotic, disorganized or ill-disciplined approach to practice. One important point to empha-size in this regard is that being organized involves a set of skills, and is not simply a matter of being born an organized or disorganized person (Thompson, 2002a). The ability to learn how to handle work efficiently and effectively, and thus avoid chaos, is something that can be learned over time. We have enough chaos to contend with in social work without making it worse by failing to develop our own orga-nizational skills!

We shall return to the topic of time and workload management in Chapter 7.

Oppressive practice

The need to recognize the significance of discrimination and oppres-sion in clients' lives and circumstances has already been emphasized. However, we should also note that, if we are not careful, our own practice can add to or exacerbate the oppression that clients already experience. That is, if we do not guard against the danger, there is the serious risk that our practice may be oppressive in its own right. This can arise in a number of ways:

- through naïveté or ignorance: failing to recognize significant issues of inequality and thus exacerbating them by not addressing them (for example, not recognizing the need for an interpreter in working with someone whose first language is not English);
- by reinforcing stereotypes: jumping to conclusions about a particu-lar individual without actually assessing their circumstances (for example, assuming that a disabled person is not able to make deci-sions for him- or herself);
- through inappropriate language: expressing yourself in ways that add to discrimination in some way (for example, reinforcing ageism by referring to older people as 'old dears' – see Thompson, 1995a);

- by using power inappropriately: failing to safeguard against the misuse of your personal or professional power (for example, providing a lower level of service to a gay client because you disapprove of homosexuality – see Brown, 1998);
- by drawing on a 'medical model': acting as an 'expert' who decides what to do without reference to the people concerned (for example, attempting to impose your own solution on a situation rather than seeking to work in partnership – see below).

In view of these examples, it is important that we seek to make sure that we are not only recognizing discrimination and oppression in the lives and circumstances of clients, but are also fully conscious of the dangers of our own practice being oppressive. It is a sobering thought that well-meaning social work practitioners can unwittingly act oppressively towards people whose lives may already be characterized by considerable social disadvantage and inequality if steps have not been taken to ensure that this does not happen. This will be an important point to remember when we discuss reflective practice below.

These, then, are five major ways in which practice can run the risk of doing more harm than good. The discussions here should have provided a fairly clear picture of what needs to be avoided in order to promote good practice. Having considered what we should avoid, it is now time to move on to consider what positive steps we can and should take to make high-quality practice a reality, beginning with partnership.

Working in partnership

As we noted in Chapter 5, working in partnership is an important social work value. It involves going beyond trying to 'cure' people of their 'ills' by trying to be the expert with the answers. Instead of this medical model, partnership offers a way forward in which the social worker collaborates with others involved in the situation – clients, carers, voluntary workers, professional staff and so on – in order to maximize the resources available and the opportunities for making progress.

Partnership, like empowerment, has become something of a 'buzz-word' in social work in recent years. However, also like empowerment, it is much more than a fashionable concept – it is a fundamental principle of good practice (and, indeed, as we saw in Chapter 5, part of the social work value base). The practice of partnership is not new, although the influence of the concept has yet to make as much impact as I would have liked, with a medical model still being prevalent in some areas. The use of partnership as a working principle therefore remains variable and uneven.

There are also differences in the levels at which partnership is used. For example, some practitioners are very good at working closely with clients and carers and are careful to make sure they involve them as fully as they can in all aspects of the process, while they make little or no investment in working in partnership with other professionals as part of a multidisciplinary network. Other practitioners, by contrast, may do very well at nurturing effective multidisciplinary networking while doing very little to develop partnership with clients (some aspects of mental health work can easily fall into this category).

At a policy level, the use of partnership as a guiding principle is also patchy. Some organizations have developed quite sophisticated schemes for involving clients and carers in policy planning, implementation and review, while others are still at a very rudimentary level as far as embracing partnership at this broader level of consultation is concerned.

Croft and Beresford (1994) make the point that, in general, social work has a very poor track record of encouraging participation. They argue that:

> Characteristically, social work, like other welfare services, has been *provider-led*; that is to say the providers of service, including politicians, managers, academics, researchers, planners and practitioners, have shaped it, *not* the people for whom it is intended. A number of key problems are associated with such provider-led services, including institutionalization, paternalism, inadequate safeguards for the rights of service users and abuse. (p. 50)

The development of participatory approaches based on the principle of partnership therefore has a long way to go yet before partnership becomes fully established as the basis of social work policy and practice.

While there are clearly problems to be overcome if partnership is to be taken as seriously as it deserves at the broader level of policy, there are, none the less, steps that individual social workers can take to make sure that their own work enshrines the value of partnership. These include:

- Keep the channels of communication open, with clients, with carers and with others involved.
- Make sure that you consult with the relevant people when forming your view of the situation – work together on assessing the situation as far as possible.
- Work *with* people when carrying out your intervention – do not do things *to* them or *for* them, unless this is required by the specific circumstances of the case.
- Do not rely on stereotypes or untested assumptions in relation to either clients or colleagues.
- Remember that responsibility for resolving the situation is shared – you should not act independently of the others involved in order to deal with your own anxiety about being responsible for the outcome of the situation.

The point about not stereotyping is an important one to emphasize, as this can be very problematic. In relation to clients, stereotyping can lead to our practice being discriminatory and thus oppressive. In relation to colleagues, stereotyping can (and sadly often does) lead to tension, mistrust, poor communication and a generally very unfavourable foundation for the development of multidisciplinary partnership. We have to remember that colleagues from other agencies may have different:

- priorities;
- values;
- worries and concerns;
- pressures and constraints;
- objectives;
- legal obligations; and
- expectations (of the client, of themselves, and of you).

It is very easy for these differences of perspective from our own to stand in the way of effective multidisciplinary partnership. It is therefore important that we are aware of any such differences and try to deal with them positively, rather than allow them to stand between us.

In relation to building partnership with clients, one important aspect I feel is worthy of emphasis is that of 'setting out your stall'. This is a term I use to describe the process of making it clear at the beginning of our involvement why we are there, what our role is, what we expect of them, what they can expect of us and so on.

Without this initial process of clarification, it is very easy for a mystique to develop which stands in the way of sound working relationships developing. If this initial groundwork is not completed appropriately and skilfully, the client can be left feeling suspicious, guarded and therefore reluctant to trust or co-operate. This is especially the case where there may be an actual or perceived conflict of interest between client and worker (in relation to child protection, for example). In such cases, it is important to identify any such conflicts so that they can be addressed as openly and constructively as possible, rather than allowed to become a hidden agenda.

Being systematic

Systematic practice acts as a useful counterbalance to one of the great problems that has haunted social work for a long, long time – that of drift. Drift refers to the unsatisfactory situation where the worker (and possibly others involved) 'loses the plot' and fails to keep a clear focus. Drift occurs where the social worker has not managed to keep a clear purchase on what they are doing and why they are doing it.

Often drift is the result of being overworked. As one worker once said to me: 'I sometimes get so busy that I forget what it is that I'm supposed to be doing. I lose sight of what I'm trying to achieve.' Systematic practice is intended as an 'antidote' to drift. This can be achieved by keeping three questions clear in our minds when dealing with any particular situation:

- What are we trying to achieve?
- How are we going to achieve it?
- How will we know when we have achieved it?

The third question is particularly important, as it helps to make sure that we have answered the first two appropriately. For example, if I am too vague in answering the first two questions I will not be able to answer the third question which asks me, in effect, to identify what success looks like, how I will know that we have arrived at our destination.

This three-question framework (taken from Thompson, 2002a) offers a very useful way of making sure we are being systematic in our practice and thus not falling foul of drift. It helps to keep us focused and on target.

A further aspect of systematic practice is that of being able to follow a clear process in undertaking our work. This 'social work process' can be understood in terms of five stages. These were discussed earlier but they are sufficiently important to warrant further emphasis:

- *Assessment* This involves gathering relevant information, forming a picture of the situation, what needs to be done and so on, as well as forming a view as to how the situation can best be tackled.
- *Intervention* This is the process of responding to the problems and unmet needs identified at the assessment stage. There are various methods of intervention that can be used to try and achieve this – see, for example, Payne (1997) or Stepney and Ford (2000).
- *Review* The situation has to be reviewed from time to time to make sure that we are aware of what has changed or what we may have got wrong in our initial assessment.
- *Ending* Sooner or later our involvement must come to an end. Intervention is not open ended.
- *Evaluation* When we have completed our intervention, this is a good time to evaluate our work – to consider what worked well, what we could have done better and what we have learned from the process (see Shaw, 1996).

This is not intended as a rigid, inflexible process that we should follow slavishly. It is designed as a framework to be used as a helpful guide to systematic practice – but it should be noted that 'systematic' should not be equated with 'rigid', 'mechanical' or 'uncritical'. Like any tool, it has to be used sensitively and appropriately. It is geared towards facilitating reflective practice, rather than replacing it.

It should also be noted that it is an *iterative* process. That is, it is not a straightforward linear progression. At any point, the need may arise to go back to the beginning, to undertake a fresh assessment.

A major key to the successful use of this process is the quality of assessment. This is because the effectiveness of the other stages hinges on the appropriateness of the initial assessment (and any subsequent reassessments). Intervention is determined in accordance with the picture developed through the assessment; when intervention is reviewed, the assessment acts (or should act) as the point of reference for that review. Similarly, in most cases, termination will be decided upon in relation to the assessment, when it is decided that agreed objectives (What are you trying to achieve?) have been fully met, met as far as possible or determined now to be unachievable, given available time, resources and priorities. Evaluation too will relate back to the assessment in asking how effectively the identified problems and unmet needs were addressed and what can be learned from that.

It is therefore crucial that we do not skimp on assessment, as inadequacies at this stage can lead to major problems later in the process. Bevan (1998) provides a clear picture of what constitutes a high-quality assessment:

> Assessment should bring together information relevant to the physical, psychological, social and spiritual dimensions of the situation. Once this is gathered, the worker needs to make sense of the information by understanding the person as part of many systems – for example, family, school, friendship and the religious and cultural dimensions of their lives. For assessment to be both accurate and adequate, it is imperative to acknowledge the influential factors of race, culture, gender and disability. Importantly, the assessment needs to recognise the structural and social dimensions and the way these disparities impact on a person's coping resources. (p. 31)

Without a good assessment to build on, subsequent interventions are likely to be subject to a number of problems, distortions and misguided actions. The importance of thorough, high-quality assessment as the basis of systematic practice cannot be overemphasized.

Emancipatory practice

Emancipatory practice is a term that refers to forms of practice which are geared towards tackling discrimination and oppression. Because social workers have a lot of power (because of their position of authority, access to resources and so on) and clients are so often subject to one or more forms of discrimination, great care has to be taken to ensure that the actions taken by workers reduce or undermine such discrimination, rather than reinforce or exacerbate it. Consider the following two brief examples of how discrimination can be so relevant to social work situations:

- A black girl is placed with white foster carers. They have no knowledge or understanding of her religious and cultural beliefs and practices; her food preferences; or her hair and skin care needs. Consequently, she receives a far less appropriate level of care than a white child would have done. She therefore encounters a further example of racism.
- An elderly man is struggling to cope on his own in the community. He is entitled to community care services but he refuses to

accept them. He does not want to be a nuisance and take up public resources that could be spent on a young family. He has internalized ageist values that older people are less worthy of help than their younger counterparts.

There are no simple answers to the question of how do we work in an emancipatory way. Indeed, I have elsewhere been critical of attempts to promote equality that are oversimplified and therefore potentially dangerous and counterproductive. I am therefore wary of trying to present simple guidelines in a short section here. It is therefore very important that what is presented here is seen as a brief introduction to the ideas underpinning emancipatory practice and to the relevant literature base (see the 'Guide to further learning' section below).

At its simplest level, emancipatory practice can be summarized in terms of the following basic tenets:

- We live in a society characterized by various forms of inequality. As a result of this, certain groups in society have less access to resources, fewer opportunities or 'life chances', less power and influence, poorer health and so on.
- Those groups adversely affected by inequality are often stigmatized, disadvantaged and discriminated against – treated less fairly and favourably than others.
- Discrimination leads to the groups and individuals experiencing oppression. Such oppression can have a seriously adverse effect on the health and well-being of the people concerned – adding significantly to the problems arising from the inequality, disadvantage and discrimination they face on a daily basis.
- Many individuals experience several forms of discrimination at the same time – for example, a black woman experiencing racism and sexism simultaneously. Forms of discrimination do not operate independently – they combine as dimensions of the individual's life experience to produce complex effects.
- The interventions of social workers are not neutral – they will either be part of the solution in tackling discrimination and oppression or part of the problem in condoning or reinforcing them.

From these we can derive the following implications for practice:

- When undertaking an assessment, be sure to consider social factors such as class, race, ethnicity, gender, age disability and sexual identity – beware of too narrow a focus on the individual which neglects his or her wider circumstances.

- Be wary of stereotypes and prejudicial assumptions – these are both very commonplace and often profoundly discriminatory.
- Do not assign people to discriminatory roles – for example, do not assume that a woman in a family should be the person to take responsibility for childcare matters.
- Be sensitive to difference and diversity, resisting the pressure to make people conform to 'white malestream' norms.
- Recognize your own power and that of other professionals, and make sure that it is not used to the detriment of clients.
- Do not condone or reinforce the discriminatory actions or attitudes of others – challenge them sensitively and constructively.

Of course, this is not an exhaustive list, but it should be sufficient to paint a picture of what is involved in making sure that our actions as social workers are geared towards challenging and undermining discrimination and oppression and not an added burden for already disadvantaged people to bear.

One of the problems associated with attempts to develop emancipatory practice is that they are often trivialized or undermined by people dismissing them as 'political correctness' This tendency not to take inequality seriously is a powerful factor which can have major effects on our genuine efforts to tackle the discrimination and oppression so frequently encountered when working with social work clients. This represents a clash of ideologies. On the one hand, social workers working with the most marginalized and disadvantaged groups in society are likely to be only too aware of the problems of inequality, social injustice and exclusion. The general public, however, are far less likely to appreciate the extent and intensity of such problems and are therefore more likely to dismiss the emphasis on inequality as 'political correctness' (this is a point to which I shall return in Chapter 7). However, I would very much agree with Preston-Shoot's (1996) comments when he argues that:

> To work with people in ways that seek to make them stronger than before is not to engage in political correctness but is to rediscover the basis of a social practice. It requires practitioners and managers to engage in continued unlearning and learning, an active consideration of the personal values brought to every interaction, both to understand assumptions which are being made and to reflect on how others construe their world. It requires the development of empowerment and

partnership skills, rooted where possible in an anti-oppressive frame-work, which enables people to engage individually and collectively as change agents themselves. (pp. 38–9)

Reflective practice

The notion of 'reflective practice' is one that has been influential in nurse education for a long time, but it is only relatively recently that it has started to make its mark on social work education and practice. The idea is mainly associated with the work of Schön (1983, 1987, 1992) who was critical of the traditional idea of applying theory to practice, as if theories could provide 'ready-made' solutions to prac-tice problems.

In its place he offered a model of professional practice in which we wrestle with the 'messy' complexities of real-life situations, drawing on knowledge from a variety of sources, including both 'formal' knowl-edge based on research and theoretical literature, and the 'informal' knowledge of previous practice and life experience. In this way, pro-fessional practice is better seen as a process of using the 'raw material' of the knowledge to tailor interventions to the specific situations we are dealing with, rather than one in which we look to others (theorists, researchers, educators) for 'off-the-peg' solutions.

Schön emphasized two important aspects of this process: reflection-in-action and reflection-on-action. The former refers to 'thinking on our feet', adopting an imaginative and creative approach to practice by thinking about what is happening while it is happening and forging the most appropriate way forward. This is quite a skilful activity and is something that can take a lot of practice to develop. It involves hav-ing a good knowledge base, analytical skills, the ability to weigh up situations and the confidence to put ideas into practice. The latter, as its name implies, refers to the process of reflecting *on* our practice after the event, so that we can learn from it and appreciate the connections between our thoughts and actions.

Gould (1996) explains reflective practice in the following terms:

> There is considerable empirical evidence, based on research into a variety of occupations, suggesting that expertise does not derive from the application of rules or procedures applied deductively from posi-tivist research. Instead, it is argued that practice wisdom rests upon highly developed intuition which may be difficult to articulate but can be demonstrated through practice. On the basis of this reconstructed

epistemology of practice, reflective learning offers an approach to education which operates through an understanding of professional knowledge as primarily developed through practice and the systematic analysis of experience. (p. 1)

Reflective practice helps us to steer clear of two unhelpful extremes. On the one hand, it avoids an anti-intellectual approach – that is, one where practitioners attempt to reject theory and prefer to rely on 'common sense' (see Thompson, 2000a, for a discussion of the dangers of this approach). On the other hand, it draws attention to the problems of what Schön calls 'technical rationality', the belief that theory and research can, if suitably well developed, provide solutions to the problems professionals encounter. That is, reflective practice provides a balance between the extremes of 'Theory is of no use' and 'Theory will provide the answers'.

Reflective practice can therefore be seen to involve:

- drawing selectively and appropriately on our professional knowledge base, using both formal and informal knowledge;
- integrating theory and practice, rather than looking to theory to provide 'ready-made' answers;
- drawing on the vast professional knowledge base available to us;
- making use of available research, particularly in relation to the evaluation of outcomes (what is often referred to as 'evidence-based practice');
- thinking on our feet and being prepared to be imaginative and creative;
- being prepared to learn from experience by reflecting on it; and
- being open to new ideas and approaches.

This approach has significant implications for both educators and practitioners in terms of the links between learning opportunities and actual practice. This is because, if we adopt a reflective model of learning, we have to recognize that learning is, potentially at least, a feature of all practice and not restricted to training courses or structured staff development activities. This helps us to move away from some of the myths about practice being simply 'common sense' or an activity unconnected with the world of theory. Reflective practice helps us to acknowledge the important links between theory and practice and to appreciate the dangers of treating the two elements as if they were separate domains, with little or no interconnection.

However, reflective practice also has implications for managers. This is because the emphasis on perpetual opportunities for learning goes against much traditional practice in management, which tends to have a focus on clear structures of operation (policies, procedures, protocols and so on) and thus to conflict to a certain extent with the more flexible, creative approaches associated with reflective practice. That is, traditional approaches to management tend to operate from a 'technical rationality' perspective (the quest for definitive answers through 'scientific' approaches), rather than the more 'artistic' or craft-based ethos of reflective practice. The conflict between some forms of management practice and professional social work practice is discussed further in Chapter 7 in relation to the concept of managerialism.

Using supervision

Social work is, as we have recognized, a demanding occupation that requires a lot of knowledge and skills. It is demanding intellectually and emotionally, as well as physically exhausting at times. This highlights the need for social workers to be supported in undertaking the difficult range of duties they face. This is where supervision comes in.

Social work is fortunate in having a strong tradition of professional supervision that has been established for a long, long time. However, this is not to say that all social workers are equally lucky, as standards and frequency of supervision vary enormously. Where staff are fortunate enough to have regular, high-quality supervision, the benefits can be enormous.

Some people have a very narrow view of supervision, seeing it primarily or even exclusively as a way for managers to 'check up' on staff to make sure they are doing their job properly. Of course, any employing organization has a right to ensure through reasonable means that its employees are carrying out their duties appropriately – especially in a social work context where we are often dealing with people at a time when they are vulnerable and can easily be exploited, abused or disregarded. My point, then, is not that organizations should not monitor the performance of their staff, but rather that they should not see supervision as being about *nothing but* performance monitoring. Supervision is much wider than this.

Where supervision focuses too narrowly on whether or not the job is getting done, it is often referred to as 'snoopervision', and it runs the risk of doing more harm than good, in so far as the staff on the receiving end of it are likely to feel resentful of being treated in this way. They may feel that they are not trusted, not supported and therefore not valued. And this is where the other aspects of supervision come in, to help people feel trusted, supported and valued.

Morrison (2000) discusses three further elements of supervision:

- *Staff development* This refers to the role of supervision in promoting learning and continuous professional development. It is based on the idea that the demands of social work are so great, so variable and changeable, that staff need to keep learning in order to remain competent in their work, and of course to become even more competent over time. This aspect of supervision is therefore very closely compatible with reflective practice, as it facilitates reflection-on-action and, it is to be hoped, thereby increases confidence in undertaking the more difficult task of reflection-in-action (what Schön calls having a 'reflective conversation with the situation'). It can be very useful for developing knowledge, skills, confidence and self-awareness. It can also be a very useful forum for exploring values issues (which, as we saw in Chapter 5, are very complex and 'slippery').

- *Staff care* This refers to the various steps that can be taken to support staff and help equip them psychologically to undertake the tasks involved in their role. It is a logical extension of the nowadays commonplace notion that an organization's greatest asset is its staff (its 'human resources'). If machinery is your greatest asset, then the logical thing to do is to invest in maintenance engineering staff and systems. By the same token, if people are the most valuable resource in an organization, then it clearly makes sense to invest in making sure that they are not suffering any undue stress or strain, that they are properly supported in whatever reasonable ways they need to be. Staff care is not, therefore, a 'staff welfare' policy for the sake of it. It is an approach to organizational effectiveness that recognizes the importance of protecting staff from any harmful aspects of their work. This may involve confidential counselling but the actual range of staff care measures available in an organization is generally quite broad (see Thompson *et al.,* 1994a and Thompson *et al.,* 1996, for a fuller discussion of staff care). Within the context of supervision, staff care generally means that the supervisor shares some responsibility for supporting you through the emotional and other demands of your work. A 'macho' approach that tries to deny the emotional impact of social work can be very harmful (see Chapter 7).

- *Mediation* Social workers can come into conflict with others (clients, colleagues, managers), and may need the support of their line manager to help resolve any such disputes or disagreements as constructively as possible. The supervisor may therefore play a role in mediating or arbitrating where such difficulties do arise.

The role of supervision in promoting and maintaining high standards of practice is clearly an important and extensive one. This then raises the question of: what is my part in this? It leaves us wondering how we can contribute to making supervision a positive force, an asset to be used constructively, rather than a 'checking up' process to be avoided or resisted.

This is a complex topic and merits more detailed attention than I can give it here. However, as a bare minimum I would propose the following:

- *Be honest* Supervision can go wrong when either or both parties 'play games'. For example, collusion can take place: 'I will not give you a hard time if you do not cause me any trouble'. It is vitally important, if supervision is going to achieve its potential as a key factor in promoting good practice, that both parties are open and honest and do not engage in game playing.
- *Be prepared* There is only a limited amount of time to be spent in a supervision session, and so it is important that the benefits of this 'quality time' are maximized. Preparing for the session by planning what you want to get out of it and doing the basic groundwork will help to make sure that the limited time you spend with your supervisor is used to best effect.
- *Be assertive* Both you and your supervisor have a responsibility to make supervision work and both parties have much to gain from the process working well. If, however, for some reason, supervision is not working well and your needs are not being met, then it is important that you have the courage to raise this as an issue, that you are assertive enough to make sure that your own development and support needs are not neglected.

Although this leaves a lot unsaid about the important role of supervision, it should be sufficiently successful, for present purposes, in painting a picture of how dangerous it is to disregard the part supervision can and should play in promoting and safeguarding high standards of practice.

Conclusion

This chapter has explored my views of what constitutes good practice, what should happen to make high-quality practice as much of a reality as possible. Chapter 7 will address some of the problems that can get in the way of achieving good practice, but before moving on to those issues, let us first sum up what is involved in promoting good practice:

❖ *Good practice avoids the pitfalls of doing more harm than good*

- Not using routines inappropriately.
- Focusing on positive outcomes rather than 'covering our backs'.
- Being realistic without being defeatist.
- Avoiding chaos by developing our organizational skills.
- Ensuring our practice is not oppressive through the misuse or abuse of our power.

❖ *Good practice is based on partnership*

- Deciding together what the problems and unmet needs are, and what needs to be done.
- Working together in taking the necessary steps to tackle the problems and unmet needs.
- Keeping the channels of communication open and not relying on stereotypes or prejudices.

❖ *Good practice is systematic practice*

- Avoiding drift by being clear about: what you are trying to achieve; how you are going to achieve it; and how you will know when you have achieved it.
- Following a clear and focused process through the five stages of: assessment; intervention; review; ending; and evaluation.
- Ensuring that assessment work is thorough and appropriate, recognizing that the quality of subsequent work owes much to the value or otherwise of the assessment.

❖ *Good practice is emancipatory practice*

- Recognizing the significance of discrimination and oppression in clients' lives and circumstances.
- Ensuring as far as possible that our practice is geared towards challenging and undermining discrimination and oppression, rather than reinforcing them.
- Challenging discriminatory actions and attitudes in others, sensitively and constructively.

❖ *Good practice is reflective practice*

- Integrating theory and practice, rather than looking to theory for 'ready-made' answers.
- Drawing on a professional knowledge base, both formal and informal.
- Thinking on your feet *and* learning from experience after the event.

❖ *Good practice relies on good supervision*

- Recognizing the importance of supervision as a factor in promoting and safeguarding high standards of practice.
- Being open and honest.
- Being prepared.
- Being assertive.

Good practice is, of course, more than the sum of the parts presented here. This chapter, as I indicated in the introduction, is not intended as a blueprint for practitioners to follow in order to come up with the 'right answers'. Instead, it should be seen as more like a map intended to help people navigate their way through some very complex territory (what Schön calls the 'swampy lowlands' of practice). For every road that we go down, there are other routes that we could have taken. There is no one definitive answer to the question of 'what is good practice?'. Ultimately, the profession must come to its own conclusions about what we are prepared to accept, and we all have a part to play in that. However, it would be naïve in the extreme not to recognize that there are also other powerful voices which have a say in what form practice takes and what is deemed acceptable or 'good enough' practice.

In my view, the challenge is to retain a balance between, on the one hand, resisting being dictated to by other relatively powerful groups (whether politicians or other professional groups) and being responsive to what they and, even more importantly, what clients have to say about the nature, quality and outcomes of our practice. That is, we must recognize that we are not the sole arbiters of what constitutes good or acceptable practice, but we must none the less make sure that our voice is heard too, and with clarity.

Social work is a professional practice and is therefore accountable, accountable to both its political 'masters' and those with whom we work in partnership, clients, carers and colleagues. That, then, is the fine line to maintain, between the two destructive and problematic extremes of, on the one hand being defeatist and not seeking to use our experience and expertise to shape our own profession and its standards, and, on the other, trying to define our own rules and standards without reference to the other people involved, especially the most important group of people, those that we serve – our clientele. It is surprising how easy it is to get embroiled in debates about what is good practice and what should not be accepted, to try to fend off attempts by other groups to define social work's terms of reference from the outside (for example, Brewer and Lait, 1982), while forgetting to take on board the perspective of the people for whom social work exists.

Having considered some of the main ways in which social workers can strive for good practice, and indeed for *best* practice, it is now time to consider what obstacles we are likely to encounter, what barriers there may be to achieving consistently high standards of professional practice. A discussion of such barriers forms the basis of Chapter 7.

Guide to further learning

Thompson and Bates (1998) contains brief case examples of avoiding dangerous practice. Aspects of working in partnership are well covered in Barker (1994) and at the broader policy level in Harrison *et al.* (2003), while systematic practice is discussed in Thompson (2002a) and Thompson and Thompson (2002). Egan (1998), while not actually using the term 'systematic practice', provides a helpful approach to this topic. Milner and O'Byrne (2002) is a useful text for exploring issues relating to assessment.

Emancipatory practice is a major interest of mine and so much of my published work addresses these issues: Thompson (1995a, b, 1998a, b,

2001, 2003a, b). Also of interest are Dalrymple and Burke (1995); Braye and Preston-Shoot (1995); Lešnik (1998); and Fook (2002).

Participative approaches are well covered in Beresford and Croft (1993) and Harding and Beresford (1996).

Reflective practice is dealt with in Thompson (2000b) and Thompson and Bates (1996), while Gould and Taylor (1996) provides a useful collection of readings on the subject. The original key text by Schön (1983) is also worth consulting. It is an accessible and thought-provoking book. Palmer *et al.* (1994) offers a useful set of readings on reflective practice. It was written for a nursing readership but is none the less useful for social workers.

Sheldon and Chilvers (2002) is a good introduction to evidence-based practice.

Using supervision is addressed in Thompson (2002a), but for a fuller treatment of supervision in social care, see Morrison (2000). Curtis and Metcalf (1992) is also a good introduction to the subject. Thompson *et al.* (1994a) is written with practice teachers in mind, but none the less has a lot of useful material relating to supervision issues.

Exercise 6

Reflective practice, as we have seen, involves both reflection-in-action and reflection-on-action. For the purposes of this exercise, we are going to concentrate on reflection-on-action. Think about a recent situation where you tried to help someone in some way (in a personal or professional capacity) and then answer the questions below:

- What did you do?
- In dealing with the situation, what did you do that was helpful?
- What, with hindsight, could you have done better in the situation?
- What have you learned from this situation that will help you in future?

Use the space below to make some notes.

7
Facing the challenge

Introduction

Schön, in his work on reflective practice, writes of the 'messiness' of practice, the complexity, ambiguity and uncertainty of day-to-day reality for practitioners. He contrasts this with the 'high ground' of theory and research, where it is so much easier to gain an overview, to see the connections and patterns and to be able to make sense of the recurring themes and issues. However, when it comes to 'applying' the insights from the high ground to the 'swampy lowlands' of practice, life becomes much more complex and far less accommodating. We may experience the classic barrier of finding that what seemed relatively straightforward in principle proves far more complex in reality.

It has to be recognized, then, that what seems reasonably clear and helpful in a classroom or when reading a book (including this one!), suddenly becomes far more confusing and difficult to deal with when faced in the cold light of actual practice. This is partly because there are a number of factors that can stand in the way of clarity and direction, a number of obstacles that can hold us back. This chapter is designed as an overview of a range of such factors, an introduction to some of the significant barriers that can obstruct us in our efforts to achieve good practice.

Egan (1994) writes of the 'shadow side of helping', which he defines as:

> All those things that adversely affect the helping relationship and process, its outcomes, and its impact in substantive ways but that are not identified and explored by helper and client. (p. 17)

This is intended to refer primarily to factors at an individual or inter-personal level, but I believe it can also be usefully applied to factors at broader organizational and sociopolitical levels. This chapter, then, is intended as an exploration of the 'shadow side' of social work, the range of factors that have an adverse effect on practice and therefore undermine our efforts to achieve high standards. The aim of the chapter is not to depress readers by pointing out the various problems and pressures, but rather to provide a much more positive basis for tackling the problems through:

- *Raised awareness* Egan makes the point that the shadow side is something that workers are generally unaware of. By becoming more aware of the problems and destructive processes, we place ourselves in a stronger position to deal with them – we cannot tackle problems if we do not first acknowledge that they exist.
- *Exploring possible solutions* The chapter does not simply identify the problems – it also seeks to explore and encourage strategies for avoiding and/or dealing with them. It is intended as a basis for action planning – forewarned is forearmed.
- *Being realistic* Social work has immense potential for being a very worthwhile and rewarding occupation, bringing great pleasure and satisfaction at times. However, it is also important to be realistic and recognize the many problems, pressures and dilemmas that are so closely associated with social work. Being a social worker is demanding and challenging. As I shall emphasize in the Conclusion, social work is not an easy option.

The chapter concentrates on a number of issues that can have a detrimental effect on our efforts to achieve good practice. Each of these is discussed in turn, although it has to be recognized that it is not uncommon for social workers to be dealing with a combination of these factors at any one time – to be beset by a range of problems, each interacting with one or more of the others. We should therefore note that the issues are broken down into their component parts for the sake of ease of explanation, while the reality of facing them in practice is more likely to involve a complex intermeshing of a number of such problems – life is not experienced under neat sub-headings!

Forget that college nonsense

One very significant problem which, sadly, is still encountered relatively frequently is that of anti-intellectualism, as captured in the comment many newly qualified social workers encounter: 'Forget that college nonsense. We don't do it like that round here – you're in the real world now.' This attitude is perhaps less prevalent than it once was, but I continue to meet people who report that this mistrust of all things theoretical is alive and well and thriving in various social work settings.

Part of the problem, I believe, is the lack of understanding of the relationship between theory and practice. A significant proportion of today's experienced practitioners will have completed their professional training before the notion of reflective practice or the process of integrating theory and practice had begun to become established. Many will have been schooled in the 'technical rationality' approach, and will have been taught the need to 'apply' theory to practice – to expect theory to provide practice answers. It is perhaps not surprising, then, that they should not have much faith in such a process when we now realize that the use of professional knowledge in practice does not follow such a simple linear route and that the relationship between theory and practice is a very complex one indeed (Thompson, 2000b).

It is also perhaps fair to say that some forms of social work education in the past have not had as close an interconnection between college-based and placement-based learning as the current arrangements. The competence-based approach to placements is not without its problems (see Jones, 1996), but it does have the advantage of providing a framework for linking college-based and agency-based learning.

However, to argue that an anti-intellectual attitude is partly explained by historical factors is not the same as seeking to condone or justify such a negative approach to understanding and learning. The fact remains that comments to the effect that colleagues should 'forget that college nonsense' are unacceptable because they:

- *Devalue our experience* After working hard to achieve a qualification, it can be very disheartening indeed to have someone seek to devalue – or even invalidate – that experience by giving the impression that our learning will be of little use to us.
- *Encourage oversimplification* An anti-intellectual attitude is often based on the false premise that social work is mainly a matter of common sense. This fails to recognize the complexities of social work practice and, as we saw in Chapter 6, the harm that can be done by practising in ways which disregard the damage that inappropriate forms of practice can do.
- *Discourage learning* If theory has nothing to do with practice, then attempts to develop a fuller and deeper understanding of social

work will be hampered, as we will have nothing to rely upon but 'common sense' and our own experience, without being able to learn from the experience of others through research and the development of theoretical understanding.

- *Are patronizing and demeaning* The attitude of 'forget that college nonsense' implies that the existing standards of practice and levels of understanding are higher than those of the person on the receiving end of this attitude. There is a distinct element of 'putting the person down' in making such a comment as this. This is hardly the way to welcome a new colleague, especially one who arrives with a great deal of enthusiasm and a commitment to doing a good job.

However, it is important to note that it is not just newly qualified workers who may experience this negative attitude towards the role of theory and research in underpinning practice. Some teams or work settings may have a very strong 'anti-learning' culture, which can become very strong and pervasive. For example, I was told by one social worker that she was studying for a degree with the Open University on a part-time basis, but she had not told her colleagues that she was doing so – because she feared being the laughing stock of a team that seemed to think that studying and learning had no place in their workbase.

This negative attitude towards college- or university-based learning is also problematic in so far as it fails to recognize the importance of academic skills in practice. Dalrymple and Burke (1995) make the point that social work is an *intellectual* activity. That is, high-quality social work practice involves being able to:

- gather, sift and process relevant information in order to form an overall picture of the situation;
- be selective and set priorities;
- use analytical skills: to recognize significant patterns and interconnections;
- undertake a critical evaluation: to weigh advantages and disadvantages;
- marshal a set of arguments to support or justify a particular decision or course of action; and
- communicate clearly and effectively in writing.

These skills are basically intellectual or academic skills – much needed for writing essays and undertaking research projects – but, of course, it is clearly very much the case that they are *practice* skills too.

To reject the value of academic matters is therefore to fail to recognize the important interconnections between theory and practice, thinking and doing.

There is also the important matter of creating and sustaining an atmosphere in which continuous learning and professional development are encouraged. Harris (1996) argues that: 'While some professionals have the capacity for unsupported reflection, the majority will require some form of assistance' (p. 37). There is therefore the danger that a working environment based on the notion of 'forget that college nonsense' will not promote an ethos in which workers support each other in reflecting on their work and learning from it.

In view of these strong anti-intellectual tendencies in some social work settings and their detrimental effects, I would argue that it is important that we:

- challenge other people's attempts to devalue theory, research and learning;
- 'swim against the tide' and maintain our own learning and development if we find ourselves in a setting where colleagues tend to devalue learning;
- continue to promote our own learning and the development of reflective practice through attending training courses, reading around the relevant topics and discussing our work and ideas with colleagues and in supervision.

Where colleagues adopt a 'forget that college nonsense' attitude, this can be a problem for them, for their clients and for the overall standards of the employing organization. However, it does not have to be a problem for you. You can resist this pressure and continue to learn and develop, drawing on your professional knowledge base and continuing to extend it through experience and ongoing learning.

Bloody social workers!

This section addresses three separate but inter-related problems, those of negative media representations, conflict between clients and workers and the breakdown of multidisciplinary collaboration. I shall discuss each of these in turn.

It is very unfortunate indeed that, over the years, social work has developed a very poor media image. The newspapers in particular have tended to demonize social workers, presenting them in a very negative light (Aldridge, 1994). This sort of negative portrayal of social work can sometimes make it difficult to take pride in being a social worker (or at least to show such pride openly or publicly). It is very sad indeed that some social workers are so wary of public perceptions of the profession that they may not be prepared to admit that they are employed in social work, perhaps preferring to reply, when asked at social occasions, that they are 'local government officers' or some other such euphemism.

It is reasonable to surmise that such a negative view of social workers can have a significantly detrimental effect on morale if it is internalized, possibly leading to a lowering of confidence and/or commitment. This is not to say that all social workers are demoralized by the bad press the profession generally receives, but it does have to be recognized that, for some people at some times, it can be a significant issue.

However, an aspect of this situation that applies to more people more of the time is that of the effect of the poor publicity on clients and other professionals who may well take on board the negative media images and use them as the basis of a prejudicial attitude towards a particular worker or to the profession in general. This can manifest itself in terms of:

- low expectations or a negative attitude towards the possibility of progress;
- a lack of faith or trust due to a reluctance to engage with the worker; and/or
- unnecessary tensions that can stand in the way of effective partnerships.

In view of the established negative image of social workers and the social work profession, it is important that we acknowledge that we are, in effect, starting from a deficit. That is, we may well be seen as not very competent or useful before we have even begun to get involved.

Another aspect of this situation is the problem of being 'damned if you do, damned if you don't'. This refers to the type of circumstances where a very careful judgement has to be made about whether and how to intervene as, for example, in the case of many child protection situations. If a child is removed from home as a result of child abuse, the social worker may be criticized for 'breaking up families'. If, however, a child at risk of abuse is left at home, the social worker may be criticized for being indecisive or not having the courage of their convictions, thereby failing to protect that child. The media representation of social work matters can have a tendency to reinforce this 'no-win' scenario and it is sadly an aspect of social work that we can, in the short term at least, do little about.

While emphasis in earlier chapters was placed on partnership, it also needs to be acknowledged that conflict between worker and clients is not at all unusual and can act as a serious barrier to effective partnership work. This conflict can occur in two main ways:

1. *Reluctant clients*   Often, particularly in statutory agencies, we are dealing with reluctant clients. That is, they may not welcome social work intervention because (1) it is perceived as being primarily of a controlling nature (dealing with a case of unsatisfactory school attendance, for example); (2) it has been imposed by an outside agency (as a result of a court order, for example); (3) there is a conflict within the family, with some members welcoming intervention while others do not; or (4) they do not wish to be stigmatized by being seen as 'inadequate' or unable to cope on their own.

2. *Disgruntled clients*   Clients often want a service from a social worker which they may not receive at all or may not receive at the level they would like. Priority systems and the fact that demand generally exceeds supply mean that we often have to say no to people, to disappoint them by not being able to come up with what they want. This is a sad but inevitable fact of social work life, but it unfortunately means that we are likely to encounter disgruntled clients on a fairly regular basis, some of whom may not appreciate the wider constraints on us and simply put the whole problem down to 'bloody social workers'.

These conflicts are an intrinsic part of social work. That is, they cannot be avoided altogether, as they are part and parcel of the territory social work occupies. It is therefore important that we accept this and devote some thought, effort and energy to developing strategies for dealing with the problems that these conflicts can generate.

As we have seen, the general public can have a 'downer' on social workers due largely to negative media portrayals, and clients are often resistant or dissatisfied for reasons beyond our control. However, problems can also arise in relation to other professionals within the multidisciplinary network as a result of the difficulties of establishing and sustaining effective multidisciplinary relationships. One of these problems arises from the fact that it is very easy for particular groups of workers to develop stereotypes of other professional groups. This can be a significant barrier to effective working relationships between, say, social workers and nurses, or social workers and the police.

We therefore have to work very hard to guard against such stereotypes. However, we may none the less be prone to problems as a result of others having stereotypical expectations of us. Such expectations are likely to include the following prejudicial assumptions:

- *Being vague and woolly* Sadly, I have come across many professionals from other disciplines who see social workers as being unfocused, not really sure what they are doing or why. What is even sadder is that I have come across a number of social workers who do in fact add fuel to this particular fire by failing to be clear or systematic in their practice. However, the fact that *some* social workers practise in this way does not, of course, justify a blanket assumption that social workers *in general* are vague and woolly.

- *Being unreliable* Unfortunately, to some people social workers have a reputation for always being late. This is rooted partly in truth (a reflection of social workers being busy people who have a lot to fit in), and partly in myth (another stereotype that has built up over the years). This notion of 'always being late' can also sometimes be extended to the point where social workers are seen as generally unreliable.

- *Being bureaucratic* Meetings are an inevitable part of professional practice, not only for social workers but also for other professionals. However, it seems to be social workers who have developed the (undeserved) reputation for 'always being in a meeting'. This view perhaps stems partly from a degree of frustration when others are not able to contact a social worker while he or she actually is in a meeting. A lack of understanding of the social work role may also be a factor. That is, others may not appreciate that representing a client's interests, planning responses to particular problems and issues and communicating with various other people involved in the case can all involve attending meetings. The view that the social worker spends a large proportion of his or her time in direct contact with clients is a mistaken one. Each hour of client contact generates probably several hours' worth of non-contact work: travelling, administration, record keeping, telephone calls, discussion and supervision and, of course, meetings!

- *Not having the courage of their convictions* A further stereotype of the social worker is that of someone who does not have sufficient character, strength and resilience to 'bite the bullet' and deal directly with difficult situations. For example, in a child care case, another professional may feel that the social worker should remove a child from home but does not have the courage to do so. My experience is that, where this situation does arise, it is often due to the other professional not appreciating the social worker's role and the limitations imposed by the legislation. By and large, social workers have far less scope to act than many other professionals would believe to be the case – mainly as a result of the legal framework and its role in defining the limits and scope of professional practice.

- *Being devious and underhanded* Although not a very common view of social workers, it is none the less one that does arise from time to time – a view of social workers as people who are basically manipulative, using all sorts of 'tricks of the trade' to get clients or others to do what they want. Ironically, the criticism can sometimes be the reverse of this – that the social worker *should* be more manipulative, more willing to get things sorted out by hook or by crook (within limits, of course). This perhaps feeds into the stereotype mentioned above – the social worker as a bureaucrat, rather than someone using their 'common sense' to get problems sorted out. Unfortunately, some people's view of what constitutes 'common sense' or what is legitimate in terms of 'getting the job done' often clashes with social work values relating to dignity, respect, self-determination and anti-discrimination.

- *Being idealistic* In the days when the term 'trendy leftie' was fashionable it was regularly used by some people to refer to social workers. Sadly, many people see social workers as utopian dreamers who have unrealistic expectations about social change and the nature of society. It is a great pity that this view has developed and established itself quite firmly in some places, as it fails to recognize the gritty realism that is so characteristic of much social work practice, and it also grossly misrepresents the reality of the social work world. This is not to say that there is no such thing as an unrealistic social worker, but it would certainly be inaccurate to characterize the profession as a whole as 'idealistic' in the sense of being out of touch with the harsh realities of the social world. If anything, the reverse is the case – that is, social workers as a group are probably more aware of the harshness of reality and the very real barriers to social progress.

Clearly, then, there are many negative misconceptions of social workers that can seriously inhibit the development of effective multidisciplinary collaboration. Often, the root of the problem is an underlying conflict of interests. That is, conflicts, tensions and misperceptions can arise because different people want different things out of the situation. For example, a hospital doctor's priority may be to free up an urgently needed bed and he or she may therefore pressurize the social worker into making appropriate discharge arrangements. The social worker, however, may be concentrating on the specific well-being needs of the client in question and may therefore not share the doctor's enthusiasm for an early discharge. Agreed discharge procedures may help to avoid this problem but are not likely to remove them altogether. Consequently, hospital doctors may continue to see the social worker as either awkward, inefficient, incompetent, or a mixture of the three, while the social worker may see doctors as heartless and uncaring. It is for this reason, amongst others, that effective multidisciplinary work must be premised on a clear understanding and appreciation of the roles and pressures of other professionals.

In order to be able to deal with these problems of negative attitudes towards social workers, it is important that we:

- do not allow other people's negative views to undermine morale and commitment;
- maintain and enhance our professional credibility in order to play a part in challenging negative images;
- are aware of the stereotypes of social workers and do not do anything that will reinforce these;
- take opportunities to make people aware of our achievements and positive outcomes (as far as confidentiality allows);
- do not take it personally or feel responsible for having to say no to someone whose wishes cannot be met due to resource limitations or other such reasons;
- develop strategies for dealing with resistant or reluctant clients so that we can continue to work towards partnership;
- make sure that we do not fall into the trap of stereotyping other professionals and thus possibly contributing to entrenched attitudes and serious barriers to effective multidisciplinary collaboration; and
- learn to accept that we 'can't please all the people all the time'.

Political correctness

Wise (1995) makes the point that 'political correctness' is used as 'a catch-all and derisory term used to discredit all positive action against oppression' (p. 106). The main problem with the notion of political correctness is that it is based on dogmatism – the dogmatic view that there is one single right answer (hence the use of the term, 'correctness') and therefore little scope for debate or drawing on a number of different ways of tackling the same problems.

It is understandable (but not justifiable) that busy social workers faced with the challenges of tackling discrimination and oppression in a society where they are so tightly sewn into the fabric of society should look for simple, formula solutions to guide them through the complexities. It is easy to see how simple rules of 'political correctness' might appeal to some hard-pressed practitioners, particularly those who qualified some years ago in the days before anti-discriminatory practice featured on the social work education agenda or those who are not professionally qualified and have not had the opportunity to explore these issues in depth. However, while we can appreciate how easy it is to fall into the trap of political correctness, we also have to be very clear about the dangers of doing so.

Adopting a rigid 'political correctness' approach to countering discrimination and oppression is a very dangerous activity in a number of ways, not least the following:

- It masks the subtleties and complexities of the ways in which forms of discrimination operate.
- It fails to recognize or address the interactions and combinations of different aspects of discrimination, for example the combined and multiplicative effects of racism and sexism on a black woman.
- Clients may feel that their circumstances are not being taken seriously if such a simplistic approach is adopted, and may therefore be alienated by the process.
- Inappropriate attempts to tackle these issues can actually make the situation worse by reinforcing or exacerbating discrimination (see Thompson, 2003a, Chapter 5).
- The rigidity and dogmatism associated with political correctness can have the effect of discouraging or alienating people who may otherwise have been committed to playing a positive role in promoting equality.

In this regard, it is worth revisiting the quotation from Preston-Shoot (1996) cited earlier, and drawing out some of its implications:

> To work with people in ways that seek to leave them stronger than before is not political correctness but is to rediscover the basis of a

social practice. It requires practitioners and managers to engage in continued unlearning and learning, an active consideration of the personal values brought to every interaction, both to understand assumptions which are being made and to reflect on how others construe their world. It requires the development of empowerment and partnership skills, rooted where possible in an anti-oppressive framework, which enable people to engage individually and collectively as change agents themselves. (pp. 38–9)

- *Unlearning* Living and working in a society characterized by various forms of discrimination, we will have been exposed to years of discriminatory assumptions, images, media representations, stereotypes, language and humour which, of course, will have had a subtle and powerful impact on our view of the world and how we engage with it. In order to develop emancipatory forms of practice it is necessary to 'unlearn' much of what we have learned (or been 'socialized' into) as part of the process of growing up – for example, assumptions about men's and women's roles in society, about disability and dependency or about race, ethnicity and culture. This can be an uncomfortable, if not painful process, but it is an essential one if we are to promote equality.

- *Continued learning* The demands of practice, the requirements of law and policy, and the circumstances in which we operate continue to change and develop. If we do not keep pace with these changes, we will steadily become more and more out of touch with the reality of clients' lives and therefore less well equipped to undertake our duties. Such continuous learning takes far more than the rigidity of political correctness can offer.

- *Consideration of personal values* Political correctness bypasses the complex issues of values. Indeed, this is part of its appeal – it provides a simple if dangerous approach to the difficult question of dealing with values.

- *Understanding assumptions* A major part of anti-discriminatory practice is the questioning of assumptions which have the effect of discriminating against certain individuals or groups. The dogmatism and tokenism of political correctness mean that this approach involves simply masking one set of assumptions with another.

- *Reflecting on how others construe their world* The meanings people attach to life events and other circumstances are an important element we need to take into account in our assessment and subsequent intervention. We need to be able to 'read' these carefully and flexibly, rather than rely on a rigid approach.

- *Empowerment and partnership skills* As we noted in Chapter 6, these are fundamental elements of good practice but neither is possible without a reflective approach to practice.
- *Individual and collective action* Discrimination and oppression are social and political matters as well as psychological, and so a collective approach is ultimately needed. This means that there has to be scope for debate and exploration of possible strategies and solutions, rather than a blanket approach.
- *Engaging as change agents* In order to deal with the problems of social inequality and disadvantage, it is necessary to act as 'change agents', to play a part in promoting positive changes.

Of course, it should be abundantly clear from this list that political correctness, as a simplistic formula approach, is far from adequate as the basis for practice. The challenge of countering discrimination and oppression is far more complex and demanding than this. As Ahmad and Atkin (1996) argue in relation to anti-racist practice:

> Reductionist approaches to minority cultures abound, and although their simplicity and rigidity hinders rather than helps service delivery, they remain popular with professionals (Bowler, 1993). (p. 4)

Consequently, it is very important that we guard against relying on the oversimplified approach that has come to be known as political correctness. In order to avoid this pitfall and the dogmatism on which it is based, we should be careful to make sure that we:

- develop linguistic sensitivity, learning to recognize which forms of language are, in certain circumstances, discriminatory or reinforce inequalities – and not simply compile a list of 'taboo' words to avoid (Thompson, 2003b);
- deal with each situation on its merits, rather than rely on formula or blanket solutions;
- adopt a reflective approach so that we can learn to deal with the complexities of practice without recourse to rigid dogmatism;
- are open to learning through being receptive to different perceptions of the situation which may challenge our own view or understanding;
- be prepared to 'unlearn' by reconsidering assumptions we have taken for granted for a long time, but which, on closer examination, prove to be discriminatory.

Stress and burnout

The topic of stress has become one of major proportions in recent years. Due partly to major changes in working patterns (less job security, for example) and partly to a management philosophy of wanting 'more for less', occupational stress has come to feature much more as a problem of organizational life. This applies to occupational groups in general, rather than simply social workers. However, there is a lot of evidence to suggest that there are many stress factors which, if not exclusive to social work, are at least very closely associated with it (Thompson *et al.*, 1996). One example of this is what is known as emotional labour.

Emotional labour refers to the type of work where the worker has to draw on his or her feelings as if they were a tool. An example of this would be a sales assistant in a shop who is expected to smile and appear cheerful even when feeling far from happy. This can be quite a source of strain. Social work can be similar, in the sense that emotional issues can feature quite significantly. Indeed, the association between social work and emotional labour is quite a strong one. It has to be recognized, then, that the emotional dimension of social work raises the potential for stress to be experienced.

Of course, this is not the only stress factor associated with social work. Others would include:

- client resistance and dissatisfaction, as discussed above:
- having to say no to people, even though we feel that they are very much in need of a particular service;
- rapid and numerous changes as a result of political pressures or other developments that have an impact on social work policy and practice;
- the potential for aggression and violence;
- unrealistic levels of workload (see below);
- a lack of support or appreciation; and
- dealing with other people's pain, suffering, vulnerability, discrimination and oppression.

Once again, it should be clear that the potential for stress within social work is a very strong one and is never far away. This gives us a very clear message that we need to guard carefully against the dangers of falling foul of stress so that we are not debilitated by its negative effects. If we are not careful, we can get involved in a vicious circle of stress. Once we become adversely affected by stress, our confidence and general ability to cope with pressures can be seriously weakened and undermined, thus making us even more vulnerable to the threat of stress, and so on, perhaps spiralling into more and more stress.

Employing organizations have a duty, under the health and safety legislation, to safeguard their staff from undue hazards – and stress is included in what counts under the law as an occupational hazard. However, the extent to which organizations take seriously this responsibility and invest in staff care and support schemes varies enormously. Some organizations have quite sophisticated, well-developed schemes or programmes, while others are constantly running the risk of falling foul of the law by not taking adequate steps to promote a safe working environment.

Another important concept closely related to stress is that of 'burnout'. This is often the result of prolonged exposure to a high level of stress. It is characterized by three main features:

- emotional exhaustion;
- lack of individual achievement;
- depersonalization.

'Emotional exhaustion' tends to have two main effects. First, it means that the worker is unlikely to be willing or able to deal with the emotional aspects of the situations he or she encounters – it is as if an 'emotional shutdown' has taken place. Second, there is a danger that practice will become routinized, based on following mechanistic patterns rather than dealing with each situation flexibly and reflectively on its own merits. As I shall comment below, it could be argued that this tendency has become greater in recent years as a result of changes in social work and the broader policy sphere (see the discussion below of A dying breed).

'Lack of individual achievement' is also a worrying factor because it too can so easily lead into a vicious circle. Burnout leads to a lowering of morale, motivation and commitment. This then reduces our chances of achieving any positive outcomes or making any progress, thus creating a situation where it makes it more difficult to gain success or achieve any sense of job satisfaction. This lack of job satisfaction then makes the situation worse by further undermining motivation, commitment and so on.

'Depersonalization' refers to the tendency to treat people as if they were things, to fail to connect with them at a person-to-person level. As with emotional exhaustion, a common outcome of this is a mechanistic, unthinking, unfeeling approach to work – clearly a very dangerous way to practise.

Burnout is an extremely worrying and harmful phenomenon, for, once it has established itself, it becomes extremely difficult to remove. Just as one bad apple can spoil the barrel, one burnt out, disaffected and demoralized worker can poison a whole team or staff group, creating a very negative atmosphere and undermining a lot of commitment and good will. Burnout is therefore a problem worthy of serious consideration in order to ensure, as far as possible, that it does not assert itself at our expense – particularly at the expense of our enthusiasm, commitment, creativity, teamwork and high levels of professional practice.

Preston-Shoot and Agass (1990) recognize the apparently increasing danger of burnout when they comment that:

> Increasing workloads, multiplying responsibilities contrasting with static or contracting resources, the emotional and physical impact of the work, the deletion of posts in some fields to meet financial targets or the demands of child protection work, apparently contradictory public expectations and vitriol from the media which often sees little other than tragedies: these are all reflected in low morale, vacancy levels and burn-out. (p. 1)

Stress and burnout are by no means inevitable features of social work, but it would be naïve and unrealistic in the extreme to fail to recognize that they present very real dangers, and that the potential for falling foul of them is everpresent. Social work is a very challenging occupation, a fact which brings considerable positive potential, opportunities for job satisfaction and personal and professional development. However, it also brings its risks, and stress and burnout realistically have to be counted among these.

In order to guard against the very serious dangers of stress and burnout, we should endeavour to:

- be aware of the stress factors in our work and in our lives more generally, and attempt to keep them under control;
- be clear about the coping resources we can draw upon and extend and strengthen these where possible;
- identify the sources of support we can draw upon and be prepared to use these to best effect;
- recognize that stress is a complex organizational matter and not simply a sign of weakness or inadequacy on the part of an individual – stress is not something to be ashamed of.

Before leaving the topic of stress, it is important to comment, albeit briefly, on the thorny issue of bullying and harassment. It is now recognized that bullying and harassment are major sources of stress (Thompson, 2000c). It is sad to think that such behaviour could happen in social work organizations, but it is none the less the case that social work settings are not free of such problems. It is to be hoped that you will not encounter any such unacceptable behaviour on the part of managers or colleagues, but if you do, you are strongly advised to seek support in dealing with the matter, rather than allowing it to persist and undermine the quality of your practice and indeed your own health and well-being.

Workload management

It is generally recognized that social workers are very busy people, with a lot of demands on their time and energy. This means that the ability to manage a workload to good effect is an important skill in the social work repertoire. It is a pity, then, that the skills of time and workload management are not given a higher profile in qualifying and in-service training programmes.

Social work is not the type of job where we simply sit back and wait for our bosses to give us orders as to what we should do. There is a considerable amount of discretion and autonomy in the social work role. Even for those workers who have the misfortune to have a controlling line manager who tries to give instructions, the nature of the work undertaken is far too complex for such a simple 'command and obey' approach to work. To reiterate Jordan's (1990) view:

> it is because situations are complex and susceptible to a number of interpretations that the judgement, discretion and skill of a trained person are required. As Harris and Webb have remarked, 'professionals do not create discretion; rather the inevitability of discretion creates the need for professionals'. (pp. 3–4)

Given that social workers have to take a large degree of responsibility for how their time and workload are managed, it is easy to acknowledge that the skills of managing a heavy workload are very important skills – indeed, I would argue that they are basic survival skills.

The nature of social work is such that the demand for services is potentially infinite (there is no predefined limit as to what type, range and severity of problems are to be dealt with by social workers; new layers of need can emerge as the presenting ones are dealt with), while the supply is, of course, finite. The possibility of a social worker being in a situation where demand exceeds supply is not only possible but a fairly common feature of the realities of social work life. Being able to manage this situation as effectively as possible is the key to good practice here.

A social worker who does not learn how to manage a situation of excess demand over supply is likely to experience major difficulties in coping with the demands of the job. A social worker poorly equipped in time and workload management skills and strategies can easily:

- make unnecessary mistakes by becoming distracted by the range of demands he or she faces;
- become prone to 'drift' and lose sight of what he or she is doing and why;
- rely too heavily on routinized practices and 'automatic pilot' in an attempt to cope;
- give clients, carers and colleagues the impression that he or she is not taking their interests seriously, for example by 'failing to deliver' – not doing what has been promised within an agreed timescale;
- undermine confidence and lose professional credibility;
- distort priorities and give attention to less important matters when more pressing concerns are not being addressed;
- experience stress, possibly to the point where health or personal well-being are seriously affected.

Clearly, then, a lack of workload management skills is potentially a major problem, and yet, as I suggested earlier, these skills are not usually given a high priority in professional training.

Although I have emphasized the importance of workload management skills and strategies, it is important to note that I am not suggesting that a worker well-versed in the arts of time and workload management should be able to cope with any amount of work, however large. Too much work is still too much work, however skilled we may be. However, my argument is that we have to be skilled in time and workload management in order to be in a strong position to argue that we are overloaded with work. Consider the following two scenarios and compare the differing responses:

1. Sam approaches the team leader to say that she cannot take on any more work as she already has more than her fair share of work. Her team leader sees her as a rather chaotic worker who struggles to manage priorities or to work efficiently and effectively, and is therefore not easily convinced that she is overloaded.
2. Lyn approaches her team leader to say that she cannot take on any more work as she has reached the level where she feels it would be risky and unwise to take on additional duties when she is already getting through as much work as she can reasonably be expected to without cutting dangerous corners. Her team leader sees her as a very competent worker who manages her workload very effectively – and therefore has to take very seriously her comments that she is in danger of becoming overloaded.

Having too many demands on our time is a fact of life in social work, and we often have to make very difficult decisions about who we say no to, about what does not get done. Unfortunately some organizations, or at least some managers in some organizations, can make unreasonable demands on their staff and expect them to achieve the impossible, perhaps even resorting to trying to bully workers into taking on more than is realistic to cope with. This is a serious situation when it arises and is both morally and legally unacceptable.

However, what can be even more common is for staff to take on more than they can manage, not because they were bullied into doing so, but because they volunteered to, perhaps as a result of a misplaced feeling of guilt about some people not receiving a service or having to wait to have their needs and problems addressed. Indeed, as far as problems in time and workload management are concerned, we can often be our own worst enemies by taking on more than we can reasonably cope with and then really struggling to juggle it all without making a serious mistake or collapsing under the weight of the pressure. This brings us back to the point I made earlier, namely that too much work is still too much work – even if you volunteered for it! We have to be clear, then, that a key principle of time and workload management is: be realistic.

Work overload is a very serious and costly problem. It is therefore important that we:

- take seriously the need to develop time and workload management skills (learning from more experienced colleagues is a good start);
- do not allow ourselves to feel guilty about some work not getting done, some requests for help being turned down – the recognition

that we cannot meet everybody's needs is part and parcel of social work;

- do not volunteer for more work than we can safely cope with;
- do not let ourselves be bullied into taking on more work than we can safely cope with (if this occurs, we have to think carefully about how we deal with this issue – team support is perhaps the best start or trade union backing if the problem is serious and persistent).

A dying breed?

The implementation of the NHS and Community Care Act 1990 heralded a major change in the role and tasks of social workers. This phased implementation in the early 1990s combined with a stronger focus in the child care field on child protection, which is perceived as a controlling, regulating or policing aspect of social work, and an emphasis in mental health work on compulsory 'treatment' in the community and the protection from harm of members of the public. The net overall effect of these changes has been, for many people in social work at least, a feeling that the heart has gone out of social work, that it is no longer the 'caring' profession it once was. Consider the following three examples:

1. People working with older or disabled people in a community care context often complain that they do not have the time or resources to carry out their duties properly and are often reduced to filling in assessment forms in a routine or mechanistic way.
2. Child care social workers often complain that they do not have the scope to do the preventative work they would like to because there is so much emphasis on dealing with child protection matters – and this in turn is problematic because so much of the work has become 'proceduralized'.
3. Mental health social workers often feel unhappy that they have less opportunity to play a therapeutic role and are more involved in statutory duties relating to compulsory hospital admissions. Mental health social workers can also feel pushed into adopting the same mechanistic form-filling approach as that described above in relation to older or disabled people.

Preston-Shoot (1996) captures some of these concerns in the following passage:

Social workers have been drawn into routines rather than professional servicing; into implementing agency procedures, such as case management, contracting and purchasing, and budgeting, rather than engaging, investing emotionally in and being with clients. Social work is at risk of ceasing to be a vision, a system of values and principles, imbued and concerned with the implementation of a critical value frame and knowledge base ... and of losing human contact as its core purpose. (p. 26)

In a similar vein, Parsloe (1996) bemoans the emerging tendency to focus on forms of practice governed more by managerial control than professional assessment. She argues that:

Control stifles ideas and routinizes practice, as is all too clearly illustrated by some of the social work which is now carried out by overworked and overmanaged front-line staff in social services departments. Professionals must feel that their first and paramount responsibility is to those they serve, their students, clients or patients, to themselves and to their professional peers. This responsibility must take precedence over their accountability to the organization for which they work. I am not arguing for individual professional anarchy but for a recognition of the dual role of many people, especially those who work in the service industries. They are essentially bureau professionals and the challenge for them, and for those who are managers in service organizations, is to recognize the two aspects of the job and frame the appropriate structures and organization to support both. (p. 112)

Parsloe's criticisms reflect what has come to be known as 'managerialism'. This refers to an emphasis on the 'manager's right to manage'. This process of focusing on managerial power has been part of a broader process of 'de-professionalization', attempts to reduce the autonomy and professional standing of social workers.

My intention is not to deny that major changes have taken place in social work (see my comments about change in social work in the Conclusion), but rather, to argue that, despite the changes and the attempts to undermine social work professionalism, much remains unchanged, not least the basic principles of social work. It is therefore not correct to accept the point made by some practitioners that good practice is no longer possible, that the pressures of modern social work are such that it is impossible to operate effectively within the parameters of quality practice.

We therefore have to be very careful not to allow ourselves to be unduly influenced by the negative and defeatist pronouncements of those who exaggerate the extent of change in social work's basic orientation. A stronger emphasis these days on greater bureaucracy, proceduralization and managerialism may well have made high-quality professional practice more difficult to achieve than in former times, but this is a far cry from saying that such high standards are no longer possible. As Parton (1996) comments: 'perhaps we have a wider scope for creativity and self-determination than we often assume' (p. 17).

One of the dangers associated with the idea that social work is dying out, to be replaced by bureaucratic form filling and an uncritical rationing of resources, is that this can become a self-fulfilling prophecy. For example, if a social worker believes that their role has now become one of simply following through bureaucratic procedures, then this is exactly what their practice becomes. This can be described as a form of self-disempowerment in which the social worker abandons his or her ability to make a positive difference and colludes with the anti-professional tendencies that have long existed in social work but which have been emphasized in recent years.

Once this process of self-disempowerment has become established, a number of dangers arise, including the following:

- important issues such as the significance of loss and grief can be missed, and resources can be wasted because underlying problems have not been recognized or addressed – for example, an elderly person may be provided with (expensive) supportive services which have little or no effect, while the underlying problem of an accumulation of painful losses receives no attention at all;
- creativity and imagination can be stifled, leading to a very narrow, routinized approach – highly skilled social work can be reduced to a form of administration;
- participation, involvement and empowerment become even harder to achieve, as the foundations of effective partnership are undermined by social workers who take refuge in non-reflective, uncritical forms of practice;
- resource shortfalls are not identified – such practice, in effect, colludes with social services being underfunded;
- job satisfaction will be limited, and so the risk of stress will be increased and opportunities for learning and professional development will be decreased; and
- the various negative stereotypes of the social worker will be reinforced.

The problem of self-disempowerment is clearly a very significant one that needs to be guarded against very carefully and very vigorously.

In order to challenge this myth that social workers are a dying breed and that good practice is no longer possible in these testing times, it is important that we:

- recognize that social work faces pressures that challenge its professional role but not be prepared to give in to those pressures;
- acknowledge that social work continues to change and develop, but remain committed to maintaining high standards of professional practice as far as reasonably possible;
- resist and challenge the defeatism that is characteristic of some people's views of social work;
- are aware of the dangers of self-disempowerment and prepared to guard against them – we owe it to our clientele to do so.

Conclusion

This chapter has not been designed to try to 'put people off' social work. On the contrary, it is to be hoped that, by being realistic about the challenges, demands and dilemmas of social work, current and future practitioners can feel better equipped not only to survive in the demanding world of social work but actually to flourish within it, aware of its major challenges, but also aware of possible strategies for dealing with these and, indeed, as I shall discuss below, the joys, pleasures and satisfactions of social work.

It is very unfortunate that the pressures of social work can so easily lead to a situation characterized by demoralization, defeatism and cynicism. This may not go so far as the burnout described above, but it can none the less still be a worrying state of affairs, with low morale and relatively little commitment to developing high-quality practice or further learning and development.

An important lesson to be learned from this is a recognition of the very strong need to work together – to support one another through the trials and tribulations, and indeed to share together the successes, the breakthroughs and the 'nuggets' of job satisfaction that are so important in making up for the pressures and pains of being a professional social worker.

Another important lesson is the need to keep a clear focus: to remember why you are there, and what your role is. It is so easy, in a pressurized occupation like social work, to lose that focus. It is also important, in dealing with the problems and dilemmas identified in this chapter, that we remember our values. These can often be a guide to dealing with the complexities and can help to guide us through what sometimes seems like a jungle of complex demands, challenges and pitfalls.

We must acknowledge that social work *is* a very challenging occupation which is certainly not for the faint-hearted. Cheetham (1989) makes the important point that:

> Resort to history, theory, research, and statutory authority cannot disguise the moral and political dilemmas which rest heavy, albeit rarely openly acknowledged, on the shoulders of social workers. (p. 34)

Our task, then, is not to seek to evade these challenges, but rather to face up to them and, both individually and collectively, take whatever steps we can to rise positively to these challenges in the hope that we can make a positive difference in responding to personal and social problems and promoting equality and social justice.

Guide to further learning

The topic of anti-intellectualism and the relationship between theory and practice is discussed in Thompson (2000b). See also Jones (1996).

The media coverage of social work is discussed in Aldridge (1994) and Franklin (1998).

There is little material about time and workload management in a social work context, but a great deal of literature about the topic in general. See, for example, Douglass (1998); Covey *et al.* (1994).

Some of the problems relating to multidisciplinary collaboration are explored in Dalley (1993). See also Harrison *et al.* (2003).

In relation to stress, Thompson *et al.* (1994a) provides an account of this important topic specifically as it relates to a social work context. Thompson *et al.* (1996) is a practical guide, relating specifically to stress in a social welfare context, while Thompson (1999) is a more general guide. There is a wealth of literature available on the general subject of stress. However, this literature should be approached with caution, as much of it is quite superficial and does not provide the sophisticated level of understanding that this complex topic needs if it is to be dealt with constructively and effectively.

Bullying and harassment is covered in Thompson (2000c), and Thompson (2002a) contains a chapter on 'Beating the Bully'. Field (1996) and Randall (1997) are also useful sources.

Work on the changes taking place in the nature and focus of social work includes Lešnik (1997) and Parton (1996).

Exercise 7

Consider the various obstacles to achieving good practice outlined here. Which, for you personally, would be the most significant? Which one are you most likely to struggle with? What steps could you take to deal with this? What tactics or strategies could you possibly develop?

Use the space below to make some notes.

Conclusion

In this book we have covered a considerable amount of ground in a relatively short space: from debates about the nature and purposes of social work through the legal and policy context to the knowledge, skills and values of professional social work and the foundations of good practice – and the problems and pressures that can and often do stand in the way of building on those foundations. It is to be hoped that this broad overview of social work will have succeeded in its aims of providing:

- a 'flavour' of the profession for those considering a career in social work;
- a guide for those beginning or in the early stages of professional training in social work;
- an aid for newly qualified workers in making the sometimes difficult transition from being a student to being a qualified worker;
- a resource for practice teachers, training officers and tutors seeking to support students in training;
- a refresher for experienced, long-standing practitioners who wish to 'refocus';
- a 'picture' of social work for those not directly involved but who wish to know more for whatever reason.

Like any book, of course, it is a snapshot of a moving picture. Social work continues to change and develop. Just as each social worker faces a range of challenges as part and parcel of the job, so too does the profession of social work as a whole. We all have a part to play in responding positively and responsibly to the challenges we face as individuals in the social work world, but I would also want to argue that we have a responsibility to the profession as a whole, and so each of us should play a part in the collective effort of ensuring that social work remains an important and valuable force in society. This is not a romanticized view that social work can cure all of society's ills, but rather a simple recognition that, if those of us within the social work world do not appreciate the valuable contribution we can make, then clearly we are lost when it comes to convincing others of what we can offer or trying to challenge negative images and stereotypes.

Social work is indeed a changing and developing entity. There has been much talk of social work being 'in crisis', but I prefer to see it not so much as a crisis (which, by definition, is a short-lived event) but more as something continually changing and evolving. Given that we are responding to *social* problems, then clearly social work will need to change as society changes. I therefore believe that we all have a part to play in seeking to shape those changes so that, as matters evolve, the strengths of social work as a humanitarian endeavour are retained, consolidated and enhanced.

In order to make such a positive contribution, though, we have to be committed to social work; we have to recognize its positive value and not be seduced by its problems, pressures and failings. We need a balanced and realistic view, neither unduly pessimistic and defeatist nor overly optimistic, naïve and romanticized. An important part of this is being aware of both the pleasures and the pains of social work, the frustrations and the satisfactions.

Some jobs come with built-in opportunities for recognition to be given and job satisfaction to be enjoyed – for example, stage performers get their round of applause. However, in social work, it is not so clear cut. There is much more of an onus on the individual worker to be able to recognize the successes, satisfactions and rewards of the job. It is perhaps for this reason that we can so easily forget that there are such rewards and satisfactions involved in the work.

The other side of the coin – the pressures, the problems, the pains and frustrations – is much easier to spot, of course, as social work is very much about tackling the problems and challenges of human existence and therefore brings with it an awareness of the more negative elements. Social work is, after all, a problem-solving activity, and so we should not be surprised if we keep coming face-to-face with problems! To counterbalance this, I would argue that it is necessary to keep a clear focus on the positives. And despite the fact that there is so much negativity and cynicism to be found in social work, there clearly are immense rewards to be gained from being involved in the profession. These include:

- *Making a positive difference* Although successful outcomes are not necessarily a day-to-day occurrence in social work, those that do occur can be so valuable that they motivate us to keep going. Also, given their relative scarcity, they can be immensely rewarding.

- *Preventing things getting worse* Another way of looking at the situation is to recognize that, in many cases, preventing the situation from deteriorating further is, in itself, a significant success and therefore a potential source of great satisfaction.

- *Partnership and teamwork* Social work involves working with other people which, of course, brings frustrations, but also brings, potentially at least, great pleasures and satisfactions. Positive teamwork can be a great source of joy.

- *Safeguarding rights* Social work is one of the 'caring' professions, but also has a focus beyond caring alone, namely in the safeguarding of rights. In dealing with people who are socially marginalized and disadvantaged, social workers can often play a role in protecting them from abuse and oppression and the disregard of their rights.

- *Facing up to problems* Many people seek to get through life by turning their backs on any problems that may arise. This is something that social workers cannot afford to do. Having the courage and skills to tackle problems and deal with them as positively and effectively as possible is a great strength and one that social work clearly helps to develop.

- *Personal and professional development* Social work offers plentiful opportunities for learning, both at a professional level in terms of knowledge and skills and at a personal level in terms of self-awareness, a critical social awareness, interpersonal skills and confidence.

Whether or not the positive rewards and satisfactions outweigh the pains and frustrations is, of course, a matter for each individual to decide. What should be clear, however, is that there are many positives that 'go with the territory' as far as social work is concerned. Perhaps the greatest challenge, therefore, is to find a way forward which succeeds in keeping the negatives to a minimum and making the most of the positives. Indeed, as I have already suggested, it is so very easy to be drawn into the pressures and problems and to lose sight of the other side of the coin – the warmth, compassion and humanity that make social work a worthwhile endeavour despite its intrinsic anguish and distress.

Social work has an important part to play in helping to 'humanize' a society in which the human dimension is so easily lost beneath the pressures of a fast-moving world riven by conflicts, discrimination, oppression and driven by the pursuit of power and wealth – often at the expense of other important aspects of life, such as compassion, a shared sense of humanity and spiritual fulfilment. Of course, social work can play only a small part in this, but that small part can certainly be a significant and worthwhile one.

Appendix:
internet resources

These web addresses are available on the book's website @ www. palgrave.com/

Child care

Barnardo's	www.barnardos.org.uk
Childhouse	www.childhouse.uio/no
NSPCC	www.nspcc.org.uk
Child Poverty Action Group	www.cpag.org.uk
ChildData	www.oxmill.com/childdata/ ncb.org.uk
British Association for the Study and Prevention of Child Abuse	www.baspcan.org.uk

Crime and justice

NACRO	www.nacro.org.uk

Disability

Disability Rights Commission	www.drc-gb.org
DISS – National Database of Disability Organisations	www.diss.org.uk
Royal National Institute for Deaf People	www.rnid.org.uk
Royal National Institute for the Blind	www.rnib.org.uk

Equality and diversity

Commission for Racial Equality	www.cre.org.uk
Disability Rights Commission	www.drc-gb.org
Equal Opportunities Commission	www.eoc.org.uk
DIALOG	www.lg-employers.gov.uk/ diversity

ACAS	www.acas.co.uk
Age Positive	www.agepositive.gov.uk
Stonewall	www.stonewall.org.uk
Anti-Racist Social Work Page	www.stthomasu.ca/academic/ scwk/clews3753.htm
Trades Union Congress	www.tuc.org.uk
Lesbian and Gay Employment Rights	www.lager.dircon.co.uk

Law and policy

Home Office Human Rights Unit	www.dca.gov.uk/hract/ hramenu
Social Policy Research Unit	www.york.ac.uk/inst/spru/
Social Policy Net	www.socialpolicy.net
Social Issues	www.socialissues.co.uk
Introduction to Social Policy	www2.rgu.ac.uk/publicpolicy/ socialpolicy.htm

Learning disability

British Institute for Learning Disabilities	www.bild.org.uk
Disability Rights Commission	www.drc-gb.org
National Autistic Society	www.nas.org.uk
Values into Action	www.viauk.org

Local government

IDEA	www.idea.gov.uk
UK Online	www.ukonline.gov.uk
Info for Local Government	www.info4localgov.gov.uk

Loss and grief

End of life issues	www.endoflifeissues.org.uk
International Work Group on Death, Dying and Bereavement	http://maxwell.psyc.memphis. edu/iwg/iwgimports/iwg.html
Growth House	www.growthhouse.org

Management and organization

Chartered Institute of Personnel and Development	www.cipd.co.uk
humansolutions (staff support)	www.humansolutions.org.uk

Institute of Training and
   Occupational Learning   www.traininginstitute.co.uk
Training Organization for Personal
   Social Services (TOPSS)   www.topss.org.uk

Mental health
Depression Alliance   www.depressionalliance.org
Institute of Mental Health Act
   Practitioners   www.markwalton.net
MIND   www.mind.org.uk

Older people
Age Concern   www.ace.org.uk
Age Positive   www.agepositive.gov.uk
The Alzheimer's Disease Society   www.alzheimers.org.uk
Elderweb   www.elderweb.com
Centre for Policy on Ageing   www.cpa.org.uk
Ageinfo   www.cpa.org.uk/ageinfo/
                        ageinfo2.html

Social work organizations
British Association of Social
   Workers   www.basw.co.uk
Care Council for Wales   www.ccwales.org.uk
General Social Care Council   www.gscc.org.uk
Northern Ireland Social Care
   Council   www.niscc.info
Scottish Social Services Council   www.sssc.uk.com
Social Care Association   www.socialcare.assoc.com
Social Care Institute for Excellence www.scie.org.uk
International Federation of Social
   Workers   www.ifsw.org

Social work publications
British Journal of Social Work   www.bjsw.oupjournals.org
Care and Health   www.careandhealth.com
Community Care   www.communitycare.co.uk

Other sources of information
British Psychological Society   www.bps.org.uk
Carers Online   www.carersonline.org.uk

Virtual Social Work	www.virtualsocialwork.co.uk
University of Central Lancashire	www.uclan.ac.uk/facs/health/ socwork/swonweb/index.htm
Social Service Information Gateway	www.sosig.ac.uk

References

Abercrombie, N. and Warde, A. with Soothill, K., Urry, J. and Walby, S. (2000) *Contemporary British Society,* 3rd edn, Cambridge, Polity.

Adams, R., Dominelli, L. and Payne, M. (eds) (2002) *Social Work: Themes, Issues and Critical Debates,* 2nd edn, Basingstoke, Palgrave Macmillan.

Ahmad, W. I. U. and Atkin, K. (eds) (1996) *'Race' and Community Care,* Buckingham, Open University Press.

Alcock, P. (1993) *Understanding Poverty,* London, Macmillan – now Palgrave Macmillan.

Alcock, P. (1996) *Social Policy in Britain: Themes and Issues,* London, Macmillan – now Palgrave Macmillan.

Aldridge, M. (1994) *Making Social Work News,* London, Routledge.

Atkin, K. and Rollings, J. (1996) 'Looking After their Own? Family Care-giving Among Asian and Afro-Caribbean Communities', in Ahmad and Atkin (1996).

Baillie, D., Cameron, K., Cull, L-A., Roche, J. and West, J. (2003) *Social Work and the Law in Scotland*, Basingstoke, Palgrave Macmillan.

Baldock, J, Manning, N. and Vickerstaff, S. (eds) (2003) *Social Policy,* 2nd edn, Oxford, Oxford University Press.

Ball, C. and McDonald, A. (2002) *Law for Social Workers,* 4th edn, Aldershot, Ashgate.

Banks, S. (1995) *Ethics and Values in Social Work,* London, Macmillan – now Palgrave Macmillan.

Barker, V. (1994) *Promoting Partnerships Through Consultation,* Lyme Regis, Russell House Publishing.

Barnes, P. (ed.) (1995) *Personal, Social and Emotional Development of Children,* Oxford, Blackwell.

Baron, R.J., Kerr, N. and Miller, N. (1992) *Group Process, Group Decision, Group Action,* Buckingham, Open University Press.

Barry, M. and Hallett, C. (1998) *Social Exclusion and Social Work: Issues of Theory, Policy and Practice,* Lyme Regis, Russell House Publishing.

Bates, J. (1995) 'Social Work and Information Technology: Issues and Dilemmas', *International Perspectives in Social Work,* 1.

Beresford, P. and Croft, S. (1993) *Citizen Involvement: A Practical Guide for Change,* London, Macmillan – now Palgrave Macmillan.

Bevan, D. (1998) 'Death, Dying and Inequality', *Care: the Journal of Practice and Development,* 7(1).

Biestek, F. P. (1961) *The Casework Relationship,* London, Allen and Unwin.

Blakemore, K. (1998) *Social Policy: An Introduction,* Buckingham, Open University Press.

Bono, E. de (1983) *Atlas of Management Thinking,* Harmondsworth, Penguin.

Bowler, I. (1993) ' "They're Not the Same as Us", Midwives' Stereotypes of South Asian Maternity Patients', *Sociology of Health and Illness,* 15(2).

Braye, S. and Preston-Shoot, M. (1995) *Empowering Practice in Social Care,* Buckingham, Open University Press.

Braye, S. and Preston-Shoot, M. (1997) *Practising Social Work Law,* 2nd edn, London, Macmillan – now Palgrave Macmillan.

Brayne, H., Martin, G. and Carr, H. (2001) *Law for Social Workers,* 7th edn, Oxford, Oxford University Press.

Brechin, A. Brown, H. and Eby, M.A. (eds) (2000) *Critical Practices in Health and Social Care,* London, Sage.

Brewer, C. and Lait, J. (1982) *Can Social Work Survive?* London, Temple Smith.

Brown, A. (1992) *Groupwork,* 3rd edn, Aldershot, Arena.

Brown, G. W. and Harris, T. (1978) *The Social Origins of Depression,* London, Tavistock.

Brown, H. C. (1998) *Social Work and Sexuality: Working with Lesbians and Gay Men,* London, Macmillan – now Palgrave Macmillan.

Carter, P., Jeffs, T. and Smith, M. K. (eds) (1995) *Social Working,* London, Macmillan – now Palgrave Macmillan.

CCETSW (1996) *Rules and Requirements for the Diploma in Social Work: CCETSW Paper 30,* Second Revision, London, Central Council for Education and Training in Social Work.

CCETSW (1998) *Assuring Quality for Practice Teaching,* London, Central Council for Education and Training in Social Work.

Cheetham, J. (1989) 'Values in Action', in Shardlow (1989).

Clarke, J. (ed.) (1993) *A Crisis in Care: Challenges to Social Work,* London, Sage.

Cooper, J. and Vernon, S. (1996) *Disability and the Law,* London, Jessica Kingsley.

Covey, S., Merrill, R. and Merrill, R. (1994) *First Things First,* London, Simon & Schuster.

Croft, S. and Beresford, P. (1994) 'A Participatory Approach to Social Work', in Hanvey and Philpot (1994).

Curtis, C. and Metcalf, J. (1992) *Becoming a Care Supervisor,* London, Churchill Livingstone.

Dalley, G. (1993) 'Professional Ideology or Organizational Tribalism: The Health Service – Social Work Divide', in Walmsley *et al.* (1993).

Dalrymple, J. and Burke, B. (1995) *Anti-Oppressive Practice, Social Care and the Law,* Buckingham, Open University Press.

Davenport, G. C. (1994) *An Introduction to Child Development,* 2nd edn, London, Collins.

Davies, M. (ed.) (1991) *The Sociology of Social Work,* London, Routledge.

Davies, M. (1994) *The Essential Social Worker,* 3rd edn, Aldershot, Arena.

Davies, M. (ed.) (2002) *The Blackwell Companion to Social Work,* 2nd edn, Oxford, Blackwell.

Doel, M. and Sawdon, C. (1999) *The Essential Groupworker: Teaching and Learning Creative Groupwork,* London, Jessica Kingsley.

Douglass, M. (1998) *ABC Time Tips,* London, McGraw-Hill.

Downie, R. S. and Telfer, E. (1969) *Respect for Persons,* London, Allen & Unwin.

Durkin, K. (1995) *Developmental Social Psychology: From Infancy to Old Age,* Oxford, Blackwell.

Egan, G. (1977) *You and Me: The Skills of Communicating and Relating to Others,* Monterey, CA, Brooks/Cole.

Egan, G. (1994) *The Skilled Helper: A Problem Management Approach to Helping,* 5th edn, Pacific Grove, CA, Brooks/Cole.

Egan, G. (1998) *The Skilled Helper: A Problem Management Approach to Helping,* 6th edn, Pacific Grove, CA, Brooks/Cole.

Erikson, E. (1980) *Childhood and Society,* London, Fontana.

Fook, J. (2002) *Social Work: A Critical Introduction,* London, Sage.

Fook, J., Ryan, M. and Hawkins, L. (2000) *Professional Expertise: Practice, Theory and Education for Working in Uncertainty,* London, Whiting & Birch.

Forder, A., Caslin, T., Ponton, G. and Walklate, S. (1984) *Theories of Welfare,* London, Routledge.

Franklin, B. (1998) *Hard Pressed: National Newspaper Reporting of Social Work and Social Services,* London, Community Care.

George, V. and Wilding, P. (1994) *Welfare and Ideology,* London, Harvester Wheatsheaf.

Giddens, A. (2001) *Sociology,* 4th edn, Cambridge, Polity.

Goleman, D. (1996) *Emotional Intelligence,* London, Bloomsbury.

Gomm, R. (1993) 'Issues of Power in Health and Welfare', in Walmsley *et al.* (1993).

Gould, N. (1996) 'Introduction: Social Work Education and the "Crisis of the Professions"', in Gould and Taylor (1996).

Gould, N. and Taylor, I. (eds) (1996) *Reflective Learning for Social Work,* Aldershot, Arena.

Griffiths, A. and Roberts, G. (eds) (1995) *The Law and Elderly People,* 2nd edn, London, Routledge.

Griffiths, R. (1988) *Community Care: An Agenda for Action,* London, HMSO.

Griseri, P. (1998) *Managing Values: Ethical Change in Organisations,* London, Macmillan – now Palgrave Macmillan.

Halmos, P. (1965) *The Faith of the Counsellors,* London, Constable.

Ham, C. and Hill, R. (1993) *The Policy Process in the Modern Capitalist State,* 2nd edn, London, Harvester Wheatsheaf.

Hanvey, C. and Philpot, T. (eds) (1994) *Practising Social Work,* London, Routledge.

Harding, T. and Beresford, P. (1996) *The Standards We Expect: What Service Users and Carers Want From Social Services Workers,* London, National Institute for Social Work.

Harris, A. (1996) 'Learning from Experience and Reflection in Social Work Education', in Gould and Taylor (1996).

Harris, R. and Webb, D. (1987) *Welfare, Power and Juvenile Justice: The Social Control of Delinquent Youth,* London, Tavistock.

Harrison, R., Mann, G., Murphy, M., Taylor, A. and Thompson, N. (2003) *Partnership Made Painless,* Lyme Regis, Russell House Publishing.

Heron, J. (2001) *Helping the Client: A Creative Practical Guide,* 5th edn, London, Sage.

Hoggett, B. (1996) *Mental Health Law,* London, Sweet and Maxwell.

Hopkins, G. (1999a) *The Write Stuff: A Guide to Effective Writing in Social Care and Related Fields,* Lyme Regis, Russell House Publishing.

Hopkins, G. (1999b) *Plain English for Social Services: A Guide to Better Communication,* Lyme Regis, Russell House Publishing.

Hugman, R. and Smith, D. (eds) (1995) *Ethical Issues in Social Work,* London, Routledge.

Hulley, T. and Clarke, J. (1991) 'Social Problems: Social Construction and Social Causation', in Loney *et al.* (1991).

Humphries, B. (ed.) (1996) *Critical Perspectives on Empowerment,* Birmingham, Venture Press.

Johnson, D. W. (1993) *Reaching Out: Interpersonal Effectiveness and Self-actualization,* 5th edn, London, Allyn & Bacon.

Jones, C. (1996) 'Anti-intellectualism and the Peculiarities of British Social Work Education', in Parton (1996).

Jordan, B. (1979) *Helping in Social Work,* London, Routledge & Kegan Paul.

Jordan, B. (1990) *Social Work in an Unjust Society,* London, Harvester Wheatsheaf.

Kant, I. (1785) 'Groundwork of the Metaphysics of Morals', in Paton (1948).

Kemshall, H. and Pritchard, J. (eds) (1996) *Good Practice in Risk Assessment and Risk Management,* London, Jessica Kingsley.

La Valle, I. and Lyons, K. (1996) 'The Social Worker Speaks: 1 – Perceptions of Recent Changes in British Social Work', *Practice,* 8(2).

Lešnik, B. (ed.) (1997) *Change in Social Work,* Aldershot, Arena.

Lešnik, B. (ed.) (1998) *Countering Discrimination in Social Work,* Aldershot, Arena.

Lešnik, B. (ed.) (1999) *Social Work and the State,* Brighton, Pavilion Publishing.

Lipsitz, J. (1980) *Growing Up Forgotten,* London, Transaction Books.

Lister, R. (1997) *Citizenship: Feminist Perspectives,* London, Macmillan – now Palgrave Macmillan.

Loney, M., Bocock, R., Clarke, J., Cochrane, A., Graham, P. and Wilson, M. (1991) *The State or the Market: Politics and Welfare in Contemporary Britain,* 2nd edn, London, Sage.

Martyn, H. (ed.) (2000) *Developing Reflective Practice: Making Sense of Social Work in a World of Change,* Bristol, The Policy Press.

May, M., Page, R. and Brunsdon, E. (eds) (2001) *Understanding Social Problems: Issues in Social Policy,* Oxford, Blackwell.

Merlevede, P.E., Bridoux, D. and Vandamme, R. (2001) *Seven Steps to Emotional Intelligence,* Carmarthen, Crown House Publishing.

Mills, C. W. (1959) *The Sociological Imagination,* New York, Oxford University Press.

Milner, J. and O'Byrne, P. (2002) *Assessment in Social Work,* 2nd edn, Basingstoke, Palgrave Macmillan.

Morrison, T. (2000) *Supervision in Social Care,* 2nd edn, Brighton, Pavilion.

Mullender, A. (1996) *Rethinking Domestic Violence: The Social Work and Probation Response,* London, Routledge.

Mullins, L. J. (1996) *Management and Organisational Behaviour,* 4th edn, London, Pitman.

Murdoch, A. and Scutt, C. (1993) *Personal Effectiveness,* London, Butterworth-Heinemann.

NISCC (2003) *Northern Ireland Framework Specification for the Degree in Social Work,* Belfast, Department of Health, Social Services and Public Safety.

Oates, J. (ed.) (1994) *The Foundations of Child Development,* Oxford, Blackwell.

Oliver, M. and Sapey, B. (1999) *Social Work with Disabled People,* 2nd edn, London, Macmillan – now Palgrave Macmillan.

Palmer, A., Burns, S. and Bulman, C. (1994) *Reflective Practice in Nursing: The Growth of the Professional Practitioner,* Oxford, Blackwell.

Parnell, C. (1995) 'The Daily Round', in Carter *et al.* (1995).

Parsloe, P. (1996) 'Managing for Reflective Learning', in Gould and Taylor (1996).

Parton, N. (1985) *The Politics of Child Abuse,* London, Macmillan – now Palgrave Macmillan.

Parton, N. (ed.) (1996) *Social Theory, Social Change and Social Work,* London, Routledge.

Parton, N., Thorpe, D. and Wattam, C. (1997) *Child Protection: Risk and the Moral Order,* London, Macmillan – now Palgrave Macmillan.

Paton, H.J. (ed.) (1948) *The Moral Law,* London, Routledge.

Payne, M. (1996) *What is Professional Social Work?* Birmingham, Venture Press.

Payne, M. (1997) *Social Work Theory,* 2nd edn, London, Macmillan – now Palgrave Macmillan.

Plant, R. (1970) *Social and Moral Theory in Casework,* London, Routledge & Kegan Paul.

Preston-Shoot, M. (1996) 'W(h)ither Social Work? Social Work, Social Policy and Law at an Interface: Confronting the Challenges and Realising the Potential in Work with People Needing Care or Services', *The Liverpool Law Review*, XVIII (1).

Preston-Shoot, M. (1998) *Acting Fairly: Working Within the Law to Promote Equal Opportunities in Education and Training,* London, CCETSW.

Preston-Shoot, M. and Agass, D. (1990) *Making Sense of Social Work: Psychodynamics, Systems and Practice,* London, Macmillan – now Palgrave Macmillan.

Robinson, L. (1995) *Psychology for Social Workers: Black Perspectives,* London, Routledge.

Rogers, C. (1961) *Client-Centred Therapy: Its Current Practice, Theory and Implications,* London, Constable.

Rojek, C., Peacock, G. and Collins, S. (1988) *Social Work and Received Ideas,* London, Routledge.

Schön, D. (1983) *The Reflective Practitioner,* London, Temple Smith.

Schön, D. (1987) *Educating the Reflective Practitioner,* San Francisco, CA, Jossey-Bass.

Schön, D. (1992) 'The Crisis of Professional Knowledge and the Pursuit of an Epistemology of Practice', *Journal of Interprofessional Care*, 6(1).

Shardlow, S. (ed.) (1989) *The Values of Change in Social Work,* London, Routledge.

Shardlow, S. (2002a) 'Values, Ethics and Social Work', in Adams *et al.* (2002).

Shardlow, S. (2002b) *Social Work Values and Knowledge*, Basingstoke, Palgrave Macmillan.

Shaw, I. (1996) *Evaluating in Practice,* Aldershot, Arena.

Sheldon, B. and Chilvers, R. (2002) *Evidence-based Social Care: A Study of Prospects and Problems*, Lyme Regis, Russsell House Publishing.

Skidmore, R. A., Thackeray, M. G. and Farley, D. W. (1997) *Introduction to Social Work,* 7th edn, Boston, Allyn & Bacon.

Solomon, B. B. (1976) *Black Empowerment: Social Work in Oppressed Communities,* New York, Columbia University Press.

Squirrell, G. (1998) *Becoming an Effective Trainer,* Lyme Regis, Russell House Publishing.

Squirrell, G. (1999) *Developing Life Skills,* Lyme Regis, Russell House Publishing.

Stepney, P. and Ford, D. (eds) (2000) *Social Work Models, Methods and Theories*, Lyme Regis, Russell House Publishing.

Taylor, D. (1996a) 'Citizenship and Social Power', in Taylor (1996b).

Taylor, D. (ed.) (1996b) *Critical Social Policy: A Reader,* London, Sage.

Thomas, N. (2000) *Children, Family and the State: Decision Making and Child Protection,* London, Macmillan – now Palgrave Macmillan.

Thompson, N. (1992a) *Existentialism and Social Work*, Aldershot, Avebury.

Thompson, N. (1992b) *Child Abuse: the Existential Dimension*, Norwich, University of East Anglia Social Work Monographs.

Thompson, N. (1995a) *Age and Dignity: Working with Older People*, Aldershot, Arena.

Thompson, N. (1995b) 'Men and Anti-sexism', *British Journal of Social Work*, 25(4).

Thompson, N. (1998a) 'Beyond Orthodoxy', *Care: the Journal of Practice and Development*, 7(1).

Thompson, N. (1998b) 'Towards a Theory of Emancipatory Practice', in Lešnik (1998).

Thompson, N. (1999) *Stress Matters*, Birmingham, Pepar.

Thompson, N. (2000a) 'Existentialist Practice', in Stepney and Ford (2000).

Thompson, N. (2000b) *Theory and Practice in Human Services*, 2nd edn, Buckingham, Open University Press.

Thompson, N. (2000c) *Tackling Bullying and Harassment*, Birmingham, Pepar Publications.

Thompson, N. (2001) *Anti-Discriminatory Practice*, 3rd edn, Basingstoke, Palgrave Macmillan.

Thompson, N. (2002a) *People Skills,* 2nd edn, Basingstoke, Palgrave Macmillan.

Thompson, N. (2002b) *Building the Future: Social Work with Children, Young People and Their Families*, Lyme Regis, Russell House Publishing.

Thompson, N. (2003a) *Promoting Equality: Challenging Discrimination and Oppression,* 2nd edn, Basingstoke, Palgrave Macmillan.

Thompson, N. (2003b) *Communication and Language: A Handbook of Theory and Practice*, Basingstoke, Palgrave Macmillan.

Thompson, N. (2004) *Group Care with Children and Young People,* 2nd edn, Lyme Regis, Russell House Publishing.

Thompson, N. and Bates, J. (1996) *Learning from Other Disciplines: Lessons from Nurse Education and Management Theory*, Norwich, University of East Anglia Social Work Monographs.

Thompson, N. and Bates, J. (1998) 'Avoiding Dangerous Practice', *Care: the Journal of Practice and Development*, 6(4).

Thompson, N., Murphy, M. and Stradling, S. (1994a) *Dealing with Stress,* London, Macmillan – now Palgrave Macmillan.

Thompson, N., Murphy, M. and Stradling, S. (1996) *Meeting the Stress Challenge,* Lyme Regis, Russell House Publishing.

Thompson, N., Osada, M. and Anderson, B. (1994b) *Practice Teaching in Social Work,* 2nd edn, Birmingham, Pepar.

Thompson, N. and Thompson, S. (2002) *Understanding Social Care: A Guide to the Underpinning Knowledge Requirements for S/NVQ Qualifications at Level 4*, Lyme Regis, Russell House Publishing.

Thompson, N. and Thompson, S (2005) *Community Care*, Lyme Regis, Russell House Publishing.

Ungerson, C. and Kember, M. (eds) (1997) *Women and Social Policy: A Reader,* 2nd edn, London, Macmillan – now Palgrave Macmillan.

Wadham, J. and Mountfield, H. (1999) *Blackstone's Guide to the Human Rights Act 1998*, London, The Blackstone Press.

Walmsley, J., Reynolds, J., Shakespeare, P. and Woolfe, R. (eds) (1993) *Health and Welfare Practice: Reflecting on Roles and Relationships,* London, Sage.

Watson, J. and Woolf, M. (2003) *Human Rights Act Toolkit*, London, The Legal Action Group.

Webb, D. (1996) 'Regulation for Radicals: The State, CCETSW and the Academy', in Parton (1996).

Wheal, A. (1998) *Adolescence: Positive Approaches for Working with Young People,* Lyme Regis, Russell House Publishing.

White, R., Carr, P. and Lowe, N. (1990) *A Guide to the Children Act 1989,* London, Butterworths.

Williams, F. (1989) *Social Policy: A Critical Introduction,* Cambridge, Polity Press.

Wise, S. (1995) 'Feminist Ethics in Practice', in Hugman and Smith (1995).

Index